Tea

Angela Tilby was born in Nigeria in 1950.
She was educated in England at the North
London Collegiate School and then went
on to Girton College, Cambridge, where
she read theology. Since 1973 she has
worked in religious broadcasting for radio
and television. She is married to an Anglican
priest and lives near London.

ing God

ANGELA TILBY

Teaching God

COLLINS
Fount Paperbacks

First published by Fount Paperbacks, 1979

© Angela Tilby, 1979

Made and printed in Great Britain by
William Collins Sons & Co Ltd, Glasgow

CONDITIONS OF SALE
This book is sold subject to the condition
that it shall not, by way of trade or otherwise,
be lent, re-sold, hired out or otherwise circulated
without the publisher's prior consent in any form of
binding or cover other than that in which it is
published and without a similar condition
including this condition being imposed
on the subsequent purchaser

To Stuart

Contents

Acknowledgements

I should like to thank Miss Ann Golden for teaching me RE, the former junior pupils of Stone House School, Broadstairs, for enduring my RE lessons for two terms in 1968 and 1969, and Mrs Lavinia Grace for her revelations about how RE should be taught.

I am also most grateful to Mrs Joan Fisher for patiently typing the manuscript.

The quotations from *Discovering An Approach*, Macmillan Education 1977, are reproduced by permission from the Handbook of the Schools' Council's Religious Education in Primary Schools Project.

Preface

I am not writing this preface to Angela Tilby's excellently crisp and vivacious discussion of religious education in today's Britain because I agree with all of it. As will soon be seen, she is somewhat sceptical about aspects of 'the new RE' with which I have been associated, notably through *Working Paper 36* of the Schools Council, the Lancaster projects on secondary and primary religious education, and various other ventures. I do not wish to anticipate her arguments, beyond saying that she approaches the issues from the refreshing angle of the religious broadcaster, and also in the light of her own religious commitment and training in Christian theology. It is from the side of Christian theology that I would like here to say a few words.

It is not, of course, that I think that Christians should have a monopoly of religious education. Nor am I among those who appear to think that the New Testament should have included an extra beatitude, 'Blessed are those who fail to understand Buddhism . . .' I believe very fervently in the importance of a plural approach in religious education; and I believe that at least religion should be understood as a serious, profound human phenomenon, and this implies not foreclosing on questions of truth. I believe very strongly in the new religious education, as it was understood by the late Donald Horder, for instance: as involving induction into both explicit religion or the outer facts concerning religion, and implicit religion or the questions and sentiments in the experience of each one of us which call for religious interpretation. Yet I recognize too that for some people, including myself, there remains a question about how such openness can fit with faith : how pluralism relates to Christian faith.

And there is no doubt that many of those who are teaching religion in schools are committed to Christianity. So there must be a problem of the Christian meaning of religious education.

This in turn may point to Christian-theological questions about the nature of our society. Let me begin with those.

Both socially and in principle we live in a religiously plural society. Socially, because there are varieties of Christians, humanists, atheists, non-practising Christians, Jews (both practising and non-practising), Muslims, Hindus and so forth. New sects and movements abound from Brixton to Mayfair and from Findhorn to Sussex. In principle, our society is plural : meaning that it is by way of democracy committed to allowing differing standpoints, and positively tries to correct itself where intolerance shows itself.

Children know about the realities and how the principles do not always work (naturally : children are not always models of toleration). Incidentally, they also see that religion is not by school standards treated always as a very serious subject.

In brief, we have an open society of sorts. This is the antithesis of what emerged out of much of the Reformation – national Churches, official theologies, stakes for dangerous dissenters. Education has largely assumed the style of openness : exploration of experience, problem-solving, experiment, the teacher as chairman of debate – such notions are rather in fashion.

Behind them lie two truths. The first is that truth advances through debate and criticism. The second is that religion and values in general are matters of debate : or at least they are not areas of 'objective certainty'. And this is where an acute issue arises for Christian faith.

For the man of faith will lay claim to a kind of certitude – or at least he will in the light of day when the doubts of night have been driven away. Is not such certainty incompatible with a *laissez-faire* attitude to religious education? Can the teacher ever be in the situation of saying 'Jesus saves, but maybe I am wrong'?

The answer is: it depends on the tone of voice. The teacher is not going to affirm and withdraw his faith-claim at the same time. Yet he may in some sense nevertheless be wrong, for he must recognize that men of seriousness have perceived other things than that which is expressed in 'Jesus saves'. Those other things have appeared often in conflict with Christian affirmations.

This means that faith must have a theory about its own strange combination of certitude and uncertainty. There are many faces of Christ which gleam mysteriously through Bible and icon and through the lives of Christians now and in times gone by. The theory which appeals to me is this – that God transcends categories, even those through which he reveals himself, including the very idea that he reveals himself. What else can we expect? So though we may cling to what we perceive as revelation, we must always see it as the tip of a highly mysterious iceberg. From this perspective, the Christian is bound to listen with respect to reports from others on what they have found out in this brief life: reports both from this world and beyond.

Moreover, I believe that God's imprint is upon men's creativity, upon, that is, such science and artistries, and such modes of living and personalities, as display insight and originality. If creativity is assisted by independence, by criticism, by doubt and challenge in a good cause, then faith in God's creativity is also faith in openness. It is not for us to impose a wooden dogmatism upon religious truth.

Here the Christian teacher, indeed any teacher, is in a delicate position. Our schools are typically devoted to building walls in space and time. They so often channel human endeavour into the following space-time scenario:

a classroom, a period, a teacher and a class. Above all, we find one teacher and facing him or her many pupils. The result, in the case of religion, is to force a dual role upon her or him – as presiding over a learning process, and as being a specimen of the subject matter. The teacher has to avoid sliding into possible absurdities – total conceal- ment of faith; the pretence that people do not differ in religion; the notion that in regard to religion 'you pays your money and you takes your choice'.

Though I consider it important simply from the point of view of general education that young people should know something about religion and religions – for without such knowledge much of human history and experience will be opaque – it seems vital too, and this is where my argument converges with that of Angela Tilby, that the human phenomenon should be seen as directed in a sense towards the ultimate. That is, what moves men and women religiously is something conceived as lying beyond them. Without this sense of the focus of a religion the phenomena of religion cannot be properly grasped.

In the end, of course, the whole question boils down to how children and young people will see things. Here, of course, a revolution has been effected by educational psychology in its probings of the conceptual and emotional development of young folk religiously. But beyond such psychological findings there must also be the recognition, by all who engage in debate about RE, that we are dealing with persons.

It is tragic that so often we bore young people, especially in the name of religion; it is tragic too that so often RE is a Cinderella; it is sad as well that we con- tribute in so many ways to a ghetto mentality in religion. But at least we live in times when debate about the way in which religion is best explored, within the educational and scientific context, flourishes. In many respects RE has improved in seriousness, professionalism and sensi- tivity in the last two decades. If I may be permitted to do so perhaps I can quote from something I wrote in *The Science of Religion and the Sociology of Knowledge* (1973):

> What we need to do ultimately in the study of religion is to break down that simplified opposition between learning *about* religion and feeling the living power of religion. The two can go together and indeed must go together if the study of religion is to enter boldly into its new era of promise.

It seems to me that the question of how this is possible is at the heart of the present debate, and at the heart of Angela Tilby's argument. Read on.

13 November 1978   NINIAN SMART

Introduction

Religious education is an emotive subject. The words themselves provoke intense reactions. For one generation there will be memories of earnest Bible study in the classroom led by pimpled young clergymen. Another generation will recall a weekly session of moral uplift from a vaguely embarrassed headmaster. Others will have been to a religious school where they were taught that the most important part of the day was prayers in the morning. According to the law no child is able to avoid some form of RE unless his parents specifically request it. RE is the only compulsory subject on the school timetable. According to the Education Act of 1944: 'Religious instruction shall be given in every county school and in every voluntary school.' The Act links religious instruction to worship:

'The school day in every county school and in every voluntary school shall begin with collective worship on the part of all pupils in attendance at the school.[1]

It is over thirty years since the Act was passed. There is great confusion over the interpretation of these clauses today.

In a modern, open-plan infants' school in Birmingham small children are taught to recite the central prayers of the Roman Catholic church: Hail Mary, Our Father, Glory be . . . They learn to cross themselves and pray with their hands clasped together and their eyes tightly shut. In the course of an assembly on the theme of 'God's

creation' they pick up some basics of geography and
biology. They sing a rousing chorus to words written by
a Protestant. The sunny classrooms display bright posters
and art work by the children. In every room there is a
crucifix on the wall or on the teacher's desk. Plaster saints
look down from bookshelves and mantelpieces. The
children's parents are Roman Catholics, though they do
not necessarily practise their religion. This is a voluntary
school within the state system. It is supported financially
by the state, but the majority of the governors are
appointed by the church, and they have the power to
appoint staff. The aim of this school is to bring children
up as Roman Catholics. Worship and education go together. The central religious event of the week is a mass
celebrated by a local priest.

Half a mile away in a red-brick comprehensive school
a fourth former from India is explaining the Hindu
doctrine of the oneness of God and the soul. To illustrate
his point he tells the story from the sacred scriptures
about salt dissolving in water. As the salt dissolves into
the water leaving no visible trace of its presence but per-
meating the water completely, so God, though he is invisible, pervades the whole universe. The rest of the class
is made up of Sikhs and Muslims from India and Pakistan,
West Indian Christians, Irish Catholics, English children,
mostly of non-church-going parents, and a smattering of
Jews. In this school RE is strictly part of the academic
discipline. Some of the children will be taking it for CSE
or 'O' level. The teacher is qualified in comparative religion
and is using a new syllabus which includes courses on all
the major religions as well as options for looking at
Marxism and Humanism.

At the end of afternoon school, as other children make
for home and tea and television, Pakistani children of
eight and nine trudge to another set of classes. Their
teachers, who are volunteers, lay out books for them in

a dingy church. Once a Methodist hall, the church is now the meeting place of the West Indian Pentecostal Church of God. The Pentecostals let the church to the Muslim community for their week-night Koran school. The children are separated according to sex and age, and they follow a programme which includes the study of Urdu and Arabic and the solemn chanting of the Koran.

Members of the sixth form at an independent direct grant girls' school are having a debate on euthanasia. One girl has prepared the case in favour and is presenting it to the class. Her argument is basically moral, supported by arguments based on medicine, law and economics. It leads into a discussion which is lively and well-informed.

These different ways of teaching are all interpretations of the religious clauses of the 1944 Education Act. The philosophies behind the methods differ as much as the methods themselves. But all the teachers responsible for these classes consider that they are offering a valid interpretation of the Act. They are all within the law as it now stands, though some of them might want to bring about changes in that law.

There are, of course, many schools where the Act is ignored, and where RE has been quietly dropped from the timetable. This may be because there is no one to teach it. Teachers qualified in RE are rare. It is a low status subject, and does not provide an attractive career prospect for the ambitious teacher. But in the past it was usually possible to find a teacher with religious inclinations who was willing to take RE on as an extra. This is less and less the case today. Teachers are confused about the aims of RE. Some are embarrassed at being asked to teach a subject for which they have no qualifications. Others doubt the value of RE in a school which is supposed to prepare children for life in a 'secular' society.

A recent survey carried out by the Assistant Masters'

Association[2] revealed that only forty per cent of schools involved in the survey were providing each pupil with the minimum one period of RE a week. Three per cent had no RE at all. A large number stopped RE at sixth form level. Other schools explained that RE was included under such subjects as 'General Studies' and 'Humanities'. If the survey represents the state of RE nationwide, then we must conclude that about half our schools are either unable to teach RE or do not think it makes any significant contribution to education. It is not surprising that qualified RE teachers feel uncertain about what they should be doing and look for guidance to educationists and churchmen.

But recent political debate has done little to clarify the issues. The British Humanist Association is currently campaigning for the amendment of the religious clauses of the 1944 Act. The humanists claim that RE in its present form is not educationally valid: 'To be educationally valid, religious education must be re-thought in terms of education in *stances for living* . . . if it is true that the 1944 Act prevents this, then the Act will have to be amended.'[3]

In contrast, some Christian organizations have set the defence of RE high on their list of priorities. In 1973 the Order of Christian Unity opened a six-point Christian charter with the following call to Christians:

'To defend Christian Education, which in Britain's state schools is in imminent danger of being faded out altogether and replaced by so-called Moral Education, and this means that children will no longer have the opportunity to discuss and study what Christ himself taught.'[4] But the British Council of Churches and the Free Church Federal Council have both considered the issues recently and come to the conclusion that state schools should aim for a much more open-ended approach to RE.[5] They argue that it is not the school's job to evangelize. The religious studies department in a school or college is not a missionary outpost of the church. In coming to this conclusion the church councils are voicing the same point of view as the Religious Education Council, who call for a redefinition of the boundaries and extent of RE.[6]

At the time of the publication of the Free Church Council's report a leader in *The Daily Telegraph* commented: 'If there is still a church militant, then certain of its crack regiments are showing a marked tendency to fraternize with other forces, not all of them on the same side. One by one various important corps are, in varying degrees, opting for an end to the statutorily-decreed Christian bias in state religious education: the British Council of Churches, the Religious Education Council, and now the Free Church Federal Council. They are marching alongside the British Humanist Association – apparently unworried by the fact that humanists have a long-term war aim that is broadly inimical to that of Christians.'[7]

In the following chapters I shall try to explain how the current controversy arose. That will mean tracing some of the changes in society, in education and in religion that have taken place in the thirty-five years since the 1944 Education Act was passed. Most educationists welcome these changes and argue that the secularization of education necessitates a new approach to the teaching of religion in school and church. Detailed proposals have been made for the future which have provoked angry reaction. But the reaction has been essentially political and has come from those quarters which have a political interest in maintaining the old alliance between church and state.

The new RE, however, is open to criticism on educational grounds insofar as it applies to schools, and on theological grounds insofar as it applies to the churches in their teaching work.

I write as neither a teacher nor an educationist. Nor am I a parent with natural concern about the school curriculum. My experience is in religious broadcasting, an area which is reflecting conflicts similar to those in RE. Should religious broadcasting be an extension of the church? Or has it a rather different role to play in a society where fewer and fewer people go to church and the presence in our society of communities which belong to other faiths makes everyone aware that there are alternatives to Christianity? Teachers of religion and religious broadcasters believe that they are dealing with the realities of living and dying that impinge on everyone, regardless of their beliefs or non-beliefs. The problem is: How can we ensure that the important questions are considered in the most public places and that the society of the future has a chance to hear, from the living traditions themselves, some of the possible answers?

NOTES

1. *Education Act 1944*: Part II, 25, 1 & 2, HMSO
2. *Religious Education*: Report by Assistant Masters' Association, 1978
3. *Objective, Fair and Balanced*: British Humanist Association, Autumn 1975, p. 3
4. 'The Christian Charter', as quoted in *Fight for the Light*, A. Lothian, August 1973, p. 6
5. *Religious Education in County Schools*: Free Church Federal Council, June 1976, p. 14
6. *What Future for the Agreed Syllabus?* Religious Education Council, 1976
7. *The Daily Telegraph*: 23 June 1976

CHAPTER ONE

According to the Statute

Most books on RE start with a historical section designed to show that education, which was once a major part of the ministry of the church, has become secularized and has passed beyond the church's provenance. In reality the history of RE is rather more complicated than that. Christianity from the first was described as 'a new teaching'. It has always been a religion of the Word — and has understood that Word as a universal Word addressed by God in Jesus Christ to all mankind. It is this conviction that gives Christianity its basically didactic character. Other religions contain techniques and laws and rituals and myths which are passed down *through* a culture from one generation to another. But Christianity, as it developed in the Jewish and Hellenistic worlds, offered a critique of culture. The first Christians lived, as it were, in two worlds. The world of here and now was seen to be largely controlled by the powers of the age. Sin, disease and mortality belonged to this order of reality. But the Christian hope was in another world which had broken into this world in the person of Jesus. The reality of the new world was demonstrated at the Resurrection, and its characteristics were freedom, wholeness and immortality. By becoming a Christian one passed from the old world into the new. Yet this did not answer the problem of how the two worlds related to each other, especially as the hope of the second coming faded from the church's immediate expectation. Was there any continuity between Christianity and culture? And what happened when Christianity itself began to develop a culture of its own? When Christianity became one of the official religions of the Roman Empire, it became an established religion: the expression of a new culture that was both a continuation of, and a break with, the old.

Broadly speaking, in England, from the seventh to the seventeenth century, the old world and the new world met in the alliance of church and state. England was part of Christendom, and Christendom meant that the church saw it as her task to 'Christianize' culture. In the middle ages, with the vast majority of the population working on the land, the church was the hub of village life. The parish priest clearly saw it as his task to teach his people. He taught the most basic codes for living the Christian life; the ten commandments, lists of the sins, virtues and sacraments. The poor and the virtuous looked for their reward after this life, in heaven.

By the end of the middle ages there were schools attached to the great churches and cathedrals. They taught Latin, which was essential for the understanding of the liturgy, and there was some attempt to teach reading and writing in the vernacular. In some countries of Northern Europe the Reformation resulted in a sharper division between church and state. But in England church and state ended up in a new alliance. With the reigning monarch as head of the national church there was a coincidence of spiritual and secular authority. It was clear that the new religion needed to be taught. The grammar schools were expanded and the university colleges at Oxford and Cambridge were founded. This general increase in the availability of education was helped by the invention of printing. The educational establishments were run by the church. They were subject to church jurisdiction. Until 1650 all schoolmasters and university teachers had to be ordained clergy. It is only comparatively recently that the rule that Oxford and Cambridge dons must be ordained ministers of the Church of England was lifted. Even today there are chairs in theology which have been tied to church appointments: the Ely Professorship at

Cambridge is a good example. Holders of this post are expected to combine their academic duties with the duties of a canon at Ely cathedral, thus, since the Reformation, effectively barring the post from Roman Catholic or Free Church applicants.

In the early part of the eighteenth century an Anglican society, the Society for the Promotion of Christian Knowledge, started charity schools up and down the country; these were open to all children. The schools closed with the advance of the industrial revolution, as children were needed for work on weekdays. But towards the end of the century the Sunday School Movement began, which offered classes on religion along with basic reading and writing. So the church was the first agency for a system of education that was open to all. In the nineteenth century the churches made even more significant advances. Both Anglicans and Free Churchmen founded voluntary organizations to establish schools. Religion was at the centre of the syllabus — one group described itself as 'The National Society for the Education of the Poor in the Principles of the Established Church'.

The churches were also involved in the development of the public schools. Many of these had chapels. Their founders were often dedicated churchmen aiming to produce 'Christian gentlemen': 'A century ago university education and secondary education were, for the most part, carried on in institutions with fairly strong ecclesiastical connections, all held together by a fairly coherent theology. The Church of England, the universities of Oxford, Cambridge and Durham, King's College, London, and the public schools and many of the older grammar schools had a broad homogeneity about them.'[1]

In the charity schools religious instruction was very basic. The method of teaching seems to have been that of a question-and-answer catechism. The children learnt the Ten Commandments, the Lord's Prayer and the Apostles' Creed by heart. There was daily prayer. The entire system was financed by church people who also made some provision for training teachers. However, in spite of the success of the venture, in 1858 only one-seventh of the nation's children were receiving full-time education. It was clear that the state was going to need to step in. Some Free Church members were anxious about this and advocated that schools should continue to be either run privately or run by the voluntary associations. There were also those who advocated a wholly secular, state-run system, in which the bulk of religious teaching was left to the churches to organize through Sunday schools. High church Anglicans felt that the church should be the chief educator, low and broad church Anglicans felt there should be some co-operation with the state.

A compromise solution was reached in 1870 with the passing of the Elementary Education Act. The church schools were to continue their fully denominational programme, and they were to receive grants. But alongside the church schools a system of local board schools was set up. These schools were open to all regardless of denomination. When it came to the question of religious teaching there was another compromise. There was to *be* religious teaching (no one seriously suggested that there should not be), but it was to be non-denominational. All matters of doctrine were to be avoided. So while it was appropriate for teachers to introduce children to the history of ancient Israel and the geography of Palestine: 'In any use which may be made of the Bible in teaching and illustrating these subjects, it is to be distinctly understood that no reference whatever is to be made to the doctrines taught therein except in cases of discipline and to enforce moral teaching.'[2]

Disraeli made the shrewd observation that the board schools had brought into being a new sacerdotal class consisting of schoolmasters as teachers of the Bible.

The Cowper-Temple clause of the Elementary Education

Act marked the beginning of the secularization of religious education. It was now assumed that the basics of religion could be taught outside the church. What was meant by the basics of religion was open to different interpretations. It certainly meant avoiding doctrine. It was outside the law to *interpret* the Bible, but the Bible could be read and passages learnt by heart. The basics could include the Lord's Prayer and the Commandments and Creeds because all the denominations shared them. Once or twice a day the school met for corporate prayers and hymns.

The Durham Report on Religious Education – 'the fourth "R" ' – points out that there were several basic confusions about the compromise of 1870.[3]

In the voluntary schools the main aim was to make children Christians, and Christians of the denomination concerned. In the board schools this aim was forbidden by law. The actual aims of RE in the board schools were never made quite clear. It might be thought that the board schools were ahead of the ecumenical movement in trying to present a syllabus of basic Christianity. But at this stage there was no ecumenical theology to draw on. Creeds and prayers could be taught by rote, the Bible could be read and learnt, but any attempt at interpretation came dangerously close to denominationalism. The religion of the board schools was religion invented by the state, and, broadly speaking, has continued to be so ever since. Another confusion arose over the employment of teachers. Teachers were not tied to one sort of school. They could go from board school to church school or vice versa. It is unlikely that they were able to radically change their approach from one school to another. This may well have led to confusion on the part of teachers over the aims of RE. The third confusion was over the role of the established church in teaching religion. To many Anglicans the fact of establishment meant that the Church of England ought to work in closer partnership with the state over the provision of RE. After all, if the church

was established, surely this ought to reflect itself in the
pattern of the nation's schools? Was the Church of England a sect, a denomination, like the other denominations?
It was clear from the earliest stages that the government
intended to establish the non-denominational approach
in the board schools. However, there were a great many
areas covered by Anglican schools where board schools
were not set up. These were the schools of the neighbourhood and were open to children of the neighbourhood.
Yet they offered the full denominational teaching of the
Anglican church. This roused criticism from some non-
conformists, who resented the monopoly of the Church
of England in such areas. From the government's point of
view, the compromise left the Anglican church in a
position of power in its own schools and yet destroyed
the principle of establishment in the board schools. The
result is that Anglicans have never been very clear about
what their church schools are for, and what their presence
in the education system signifies. Does the established
church only have a mission to children of churchgoing
parents, or does it still, in some sense, have a responsibility
for the whole of society? This question has never been
resolved.

RE in the county schools continued to develop on the
basis of what could not be taught, rather than on the
basis of what was allowed. Some schools evidently dropped
RE altogether. A return to a government circular in 1906
revealed that Hereford Education Authority had no county
syllabus of religious teaching, and had no way of finding
out what was taught in RE classes, if, indeed, there were
any.[4]

During the first two decades of this century the situation altered rapidly. First of all there was the beginning
of a breakdown of denominational barriers. The Inter-
national Missionary Conference at Edinburgh in 1910 had
inspired many delegates with a new vision of the church,
the Church Universal, united across the old barriers in

faith and mission to the world. The denominational
barriers, instead of being the lines along which truth and
non-truth were drawn for the individual churches, became
seen as a sinful division, a scandal and a stumbling block,
which prevented the true realization of the church as 'the
body of Christ'. The Conference occurred at a time when
there had been new and constructive advances in the
study of the Bible and in the development of Biblical
theology. The rise of science, which had seemed such a
threat to religious faith, was now being interpreted positively. In 1891 Robert Gregory, the Dean of St Paul's, had
stated as his belief that: '(The scriptures) are inspired by
the Holy Ghost; that they are what they profess to be;
that they mean what they say; and that they declare in-
controvertibly the actual historic truth in all records, both
of past events, and of the delivery of predictions to be
thereafter fulfilled.'[5] But this fundamentalist approach
was slowly losing ground among more scholarly churchmen. Liberal theologians like Charles Raven and Hastings
Rashdall were looking for a new way to express Biblical
truths which was compatible with the insights of evolution
and psychology. They wanted to show that Christianity
was relevant to contemporary life and thought, and that
there was a real continuity between Christian faith and
culture. The theological key to this attempt was the
doctrine of the Incarnation. *Lux Mundi – a Series of
Studies in the Religion of the Incarnation*, was a famous
collection of Anglican essays which laid the groundwork
for this approach. They argued that the Incarnation meant
that everything human was of immense importance. If
the Word had taken flesh and dwelt among us, then whatever is human is sanctified and raised to the level of divine
life. So the theologians had to be concerned with art and
science, politics and social change. The further implication
was that in the Incarnation a new humanity had been
created. Man was now living in the age of redemption,
and his task was to build the kingdom of peace and

righteousness under God. The divisions in the church
would have to be overcome. They were petty and irrelevant beside this new vision of the Universal Church
and its vocation in the redemption of mankind.

This trend has to be seen in the light of the trauma of
the 1914-1917 war. There was something peculiarly horrific
about supposedly Christian nations destroying each other
in 'the war to end wars'. The scale of violence and suffering was something that had previously seemed inconceiv-
able. For some it was the end of faith. It certainly put
question marks in front of notions of progress and
civilization: 'From the trenches, the prisoner's camp, the
hospital and the home the question has been put in the
stark brevity of mortal anguish: Is there now a God?'[6]

Yet for those who did recover faith and lived through
the years of upheaval and uncertainty between the wars
the new 'ecumenical' theology provided the ingredients
for a religious basis to life. The new theology was basically
optimistic. Though there was need for repentance on the
part of the churches for their failures and divisions there
was no doubt that unity was the will of God, and the
whole church was required to manifest the unity of the
body of Christ. There was optimism, too, about the relation of Christianity to culture. It was essentially a theology
of Christendom, which saw the world coming closer to
God. The arts and human sciences were to find their fulfilment in Christian belief. Education was one of the tools
of redemption.

We begin to see changes in the tone and style of the
RE syllabuses which were produced by the local education
authorities. The syllabus produced in Winchester in 1921
states that the aim of religious teaching is: 'To give
instruction in the Christian faith as a living thing with
power over daily life: to put in right proportion the
teaching of the necessary formularies, and to avoid the
impression that Christian knowledge consists in commit-
ting to memory a mass of details.'[7] This syllabus clearly

had a theological and educational intention. It is critical of doctrine for doctrinal reasons. Whereas in the past doctrine was avoided because it compromised the essential neutrality of the county school, here it is opposed because the new theology is itself critical of formularies and divisive details. The church is on the way to making its own the religion originally invented by the state. The syllabus includes study of 'other parts' of Christ's church; in particular, the Roman Catholic and Orthodox churches. There were also changes of emphasis in worship. Instead of teaching children to recite prayers there was a feeling that children ought somehow to be taught to pray for themselves. They should be encouraged to make up their own prayers rather than to recite traditional ones parrot-fashion.

The Cambridge syllabus of 1924 is an excellent example of the new ecumenical approach. The object was to provide a syllabus which would be both acceptable to the churches and a useful educational tool. No one doubted that this dual objective was possible. The syllabus was seen as a positive reflection of the life of the churches. There was now an 'agreed theology' to reflect. The role of the teacher was now very different. Instead of imparting uninterpreted information, and training children in the recitation of creeds and prayers, the teacher became an agent of the 'agreed theology'. Disraeli's remark about the emergence of a new sacerdotal class of RE teachers was truer now than when he had made it. The teacher's job was to initiate children into the Christian life: 'Schools have proved that they can be the ideal nurseries of the new Biblical learning.'[8] The Cambridgeshire syllabus clearly intended children to become Christians. Worship was seen as a crucial part of the life of the school. The morning assembly '. . . will be welcomed as the opportunity for the dedication of all of the school life and work'.[9] The syllabus here is providing a theology of education. The purpose and life of the school is interpreted in religious categories: 'All education, rightly conceived, is religious education.' John Hull summarizes this declaration as '. . . the manifesto of the state school as an agent of Christian nurture'. This is partly true, but it should be made clear that there was something bogus about the claims of the new approach to RE. It sets out with the assumption that a distinction can be made between '. . . the vital doctrines of Christianity and the distinctive doctrines of the church'.[10] The 'distinctive doctrines' are clearly secondary. Yet even the most enthusiastically ecumenical Christian should have problems with this assumption. If it had been a distinction between the vital doctrines of Christianity and the distinctive doctrines of the *churches*, then there would have been no problem, since, in the new theology, Christianity was manifested by the whole church, and not, in its totality, by the distinctive parts. But to separate Christianity from *the* Church is something rather different. Initiation into the Church is through baptism. Yet it was not the intention, or indeed the place, of the county schools to encourage children towards baptism or confirmation. It was still assumed, though, that school religion would initiate them into Christianity.

It was clear that Christians thought that the new approach to RE was part of the incarnational theology as it was applied to culture. In the proposed Revised Prayer Book for 1928 the great eucharistic prayer for the Church includes the following addition: 'Guide and prosper, we pray thee, those who are labouring for the spread of thy gospel among the nations, and enlighten with thy Spirit all places of education and learning: that the whole world may be filled with the knowledge of thy truth.' Here places of learning are clearly seen as part of the system of redemption. Secular education has a religious function, and to put these new petitions in the solemn eucharistic prayer after the petitions for the King, the civil authorities and the church, confirms this view. The schools are part of Christendom – the manifestation of the incarnation. The church has baptized the education system in its entirety. But the question remains, *which* church? It was not only the Anglicans who contributed to the agreed syllabuses. In reality the takeover of the educational system was the work of a phantom church, an imaginary church, which, in spite of the fact that it did not exist, nevertheless had the great virtue of teaching 'the vital doctrines of Christianity'.

It is easy to be critical after half a century. The clergy who worked on the agreed syllabuses had reasons for their theological confidence. From the point of view of the state it was another successful compromise. As the church actually lost *power*, so there was the compensation of *influence*. The church provided a broad Christian ideology, which enabled the state to get on with the business of education.

The RE syllabuses of this period provided the framework and context for the religious clauses of the 1944 Education Act, which then became normative for the understanding of what RE was about.

The 1944 Act was a wartime bill carried through by the Education Minister, R. A. Butler. He recalls in his autobiography how, at the time of his appointment, the Prime Minister, Winston Churchill, had said to him: 'I am too old now to think you can improve people's natures. Everyone has to learn to defend himself. I should not object if you could introduce a note of patriotism into our schools.'[11]

Butler shared the widespread feeling that a reform and rationalization of the school system was long overdue. The interruptions of a generation's schooling by the evacuations, the need to create a vision of hope for the future, the consolidation of values and morale, all made education a focus for debate. Butler attached great importance to the religious issues in education. Foremost among these were the problems of the church schools.

Many of them were in a state of disrepair and were suffering from a desperate shortage of books and equipment. They needed money, but was it right for the government to bale out schools that were unashamedly denominational? This was a practical issue, but it must be seen in the context of a wider concern. For many, the issue at stake during the war was the future of Christian civilization. It was the accepted theology of the time that the war was a war against the forces of darkness. This was a view which was shared by people who were not prepared to be committed churchgoers and yet who felt, by virtue of being English, that they shared in a commonwealth informed by Christian values. It was these values for which so many had died. These were the values to be treasured and handed down to the new generation; education was seen as the passing on of a tradition. The purpose of education was to instil a set of values into children in the hope that the horror of what had happened in Germany in the thirties could never happen again.

In the year that war broke out T. S. Eliot presented three lectures at Corpus Christi College, Cambridge, which were later published under the overall title *The Idea of a Christian Society*. His argument is fascinating, not only because of the light it sheds on the moral and social climate on the eve of wartime, but because of its continuing relevance to the arguments about education, civilization and religion, which are still going on today. He argues that the ideals of 'liberalism' and 'democracy' have failed in Western society, and are giving way to totalitarianism; and that this is because of a fundamental flaw in the liberal ideal, the separation of private belief from public life. In 'liberal' society religion is a private matter. Christians should 'be able to accommodate themselves to any world which treats them good-naturedly'.[12] Eliot does not accept the dichotomy between public and private. He presents a picture in which the institutions which control public life are swinging from the ideal of neutrality to one of opposition to Christianity. The individual Christian, with his private faith, is hardly aware that this is going on. But, according to Eliot, he soon will be. The paganism of current society is gradually becoming apparent. Eliot looks forward gloomily to 'a state of affairs in which we shall have regimentation and conformity, without respect for the needs of the individual soul; the puritanism of a hygienic morality in the interest of efficiency; uniformity of opinion through propaganda, and art only encouraged when it flatters the official doctrines of the time.'[13] The only thing which will halt this rush down the Gadarene slope is a return to Christianity: 'That prospect involves, at least, discipline, inconvenience and discomfort, but here, as hereafter, the alternative to hell is purgatory.'[14] Eliot proposes a state that is positively Christian. By that he does not mean to confuse the state with the church. He makes no assumption that the majority of people will become churchgoers. The church has a prophetic role with regard to the state, but it is not expected to interfere with the business of government. The aim of government, according to Eliot, is to create a society in which: 'The natural end of man — virtue and well-being in community – is acknowledged for all, and the supernatural end – beatitude – for those who have eyes to see it.'[15] Education has a key role in Eliot's Christian society: 'Education must be religious, not in the sense that it will be administered by ecclesiastics, still less in the sense that it will exercise pressure, or attempt to instruct everyone in theology, but in the sense that its aims will be directed by a Christian philosophy of life. It will no longer be merely a term comprehending a variety of unrelated subjects undertaken for special purposes or for none at all.'[16]

Eliot was convinced that a 'Christian philosophy of life' could be drawn up, and moreover, that it was the proper concern of the churches to build up such a philosophy. But his appeal was not only to churchmen; it was to all serious-minded people who were concerned about values and the future of civilization. He was under no illusion about the level of commitment to organized Christianity displayed by the majority of the population, yet he was certain that if people were given the choice of living under pagan totalitarianism or under the Christian state, the majority, regardless of personal belief, would choose the latter. On 6 September 1939 Eliot added a postscript: 'The whole of this book . . . was completed before it was known that we should be at war . . . the only additional observations which I feel called upon to make are these: first, that the alignment of forces which has now revealed itself should bring more clearly to our consciousness the alternative of Christianity or paganism; and, second, that we cannot afford to defer our constructive thinking to the conclusion of hostilities – a moment when, as we should know from experience, good counsel is liable to be obscured.'[17] Eliot's argument sets out with great force the argument for Christendom as the manifestation of Christianity in society. He claims that a virtuous society is only possible if it is undergirded by a Christian philosophy of life. Education is initiation into this philosophy. It involves a passing down of Christian values which do not require for their acceptance personal Christian belief.

It is impossible to tell whether *The Idea of a Christian Society* influenced those who were involved in the reconstruction of educational policy at the end of the war. But a white paper published in 1944 suggests that those who formulated policy were not far away from sharing some of Eliot's assumptions: 'There has been a very general wish, not confined to representatives of the churches, that Religious Education should be given a more defined place in the life and work of the schools, springing from the desire to revive the spiritual and personal values in our society and in our national tradition.'[18]

Church leaders were involved in preliminary debate

with the minister long before the bill was drafted. The Church felt it had a crucial role in the construction of social life in general, and education in particular. In a letter to *The Times* as early as 1940 the Archbishops of Canterbury and York, the Roman Catholic Archbishop of Westminster and the Moderator of the Free Church Council suggested some guidelines for the new society. Under the headline 'Foundations of Peace' they urged: 'Extreme inequality of wealth and possessions should be abolished; every child, regardless of race or class, should have equal opportunities of education, suitable for development of his particular capabilities; that the family should be safeguarded, and that a sense of divine vocation should be restored to man's daily work.' So all the churches felt responsible generally for education, and for the reconstruction of society on Christian principles.

This high moral stance is in contrast to the pettiness displayed over practical issues. Butler had two main problems with the churches, what to do about the dual system of church and state schools, and what to do about the Christian content of the curriculum. On the first issue a consultative document produced by the Board of Education in 1941 had suggested the abolition of the ban on denominational instruction in county schools; this had been safeguarded since 1871 by the Cowper-Temple clause of the Elementary Education Act. If this proposal had been accepted it would have meant an enormous increase in the power and influence of the established church of England. Butler realized this and called for alternative proposals. There was some hope, on the part of the nonconformists, that the dual system would be altered so that, in areas where there was at present only one Anglican school, either an alternative would be provided or the school would be made into a county school. Butler supported the principle of the dual system, though he realized there would have to be some modifications because of the plight of many church schools. Basically the solution he suggested was to allow church schools to choose the degree to which they were dependent on the state. They could function on an 'aided' or 'controlled' basis, and there would be provision for a half way status made by special agreement with the local education authority. The aided schools received financial help from the education authorities, but were responsible themselves for any additions or improvements to school buildings. The church had the right to appoint two-thirds of the governors, the other third being appointed by the education authority. The governors were responsible for the appointment of staff and for the control of the syllabus. Controlled schools were financed entirely by the local authority and the church only had the right to appoint one-third of the governors. The teaching of religion had to conform to the authority's agreed syllabus. The success of Butler's plan depended on large numbers of church schools being willing to opt for controlled status. He deliberately kept the grant for improvements to aided schools to fifty per cent, which forced a number of schools to accept controlled status in order to meet the standards required by the law. This mollified the non-conformists, though it angered some of the Roman Catholics; it posed a direct threat to their independence.

Butler worked hard to get agreement from the Anglicans. In the later stages of his negotiations he found himself dealing with William Temple, who had succeeded Cosmo Gordon Lang as Archbishop of Canterbury in 1942. Temple had always been interested in education. He had spent some years as headmaster of Repton, the boys' public school. He was a man with a lively and well-stocked mind who exerted a profound moral and spiritual influence. He was competent in philosophy as well as theology, and most of his writings reflect his deep concern to evolve a Christian philosophy of life. W. R. Matthews has written of him as a man incapable of doubt.[19] For him, Christianity was more than a religion; it was a process of transformation by which human society grew into the fullness of the kingdom of God. He did not see this as a natural process, like evolution. Its foundations were God's redemptive acts for mankind. It was the church's task to proclaim the redemption of God and thus draw society into the new age. Temple was a socialist, in the tradition of the great Victorian theologian F. D. Maurice. He had no time for the assumption that religion is one department of life amongst others. If this were the case, then religion would be improperly interfering when it laid down principles which affected the other departments of life. Rather it was the church's duty to declare its judgement upon social facts and to make known the principles on which society should be governed. Temple did not share T. S. Eliot's gloom, nor the elitist tendency of his politics. What Eliot and Temple had in common was a conviction that Christianity had a mission to interpret culture and to influence it. But Temple's emphasis begins with the goodness of the world as created by God. The universe is a sacrament pointing to order and hope: 'I believe that life and the world constitute a single whole. I believe that the Word of God . . . is the principle of its unity. I am convinced that nothing is now so important, for indeed the alternative is in the long run the collapse of civilization, as to reconstruct our whole fabric of thought and practice round the self-expression of ultimate reality in Jesus Christ as its focus and pivot and dynamic source of power.'[20] The Christian society for Temple was not a desperate measure to preserve decency and civilized values, as it was for Eliot; its root was in the will of God for man's total redemption. Education has a part to play in this, but it is not the whole story: 'Man needs education, but still more he needs conversion. Man needs political progress and social reform, but still more he needs redemption.[21] There is an inconsistency in Temple's thought at this point which has been noted by commentators. In spite of his conviction that Christianity implies a critique of culture, and that to be a Christian means discontinuity with culture as well as continuity, he seems to affirm the possibility of Christendom: 'Education is only adequate and worthy when it is itself religious. There is no possibility of neutrality . . . to be neutral concerning God is to ignore him.'[22]

Temple stands in the tradition of incarnational theology, which saw the fulfilment of the Incarnation in the redemption of society and the setting up of the Kingdom. There are a number of different ways in which this theology can be expressed, but on the whole it tends to affirm progress; it is optimistic about man and his future. It may see the Kingdom in terms of a slow unfolding towards God in which the institutions of life, the political and social structures, the arts and sciences, are progressively sanctified and made to be agencies of the Kingdom. Such theology tends to be triumphalistic. The church is a sign of triumphant progress and seeks a harmonious relationship with the state. In our century this kind of theology has, in England, usually been associated with socialism. On the other hand, Eliot's *Idea of a Christian Society* attaches Christendom to a theology of despair. Christendom is a protective castle in which Christian man is protected from the forces of darkness outside and within himself. Christendom imposes discipline over his inner and outer life. The dark forces are within man as well as outside him and must be fought. This theology is not triumphalistic. In fact it is rather lacking in social hope. It condemns the ideals of liberalism and democracy as illusory. It therefore tends to a more right wing political philosophy.

Both these interpretations of Christendom have consequences for education. Temple was convinced that the 1944 Act had Christian intent. He was not disheartened by the fact that the majority of church schools would now offer the non-denominational agreed syllabus: 'Our main business is not, surely, to be fighting a rearguard action in perpetual retreat till we are driven off the field by the competition of the resources of the state, but to take care that we are interpenetrating with our influence all that the state itself is doing.'[23] For Temple, the most significant part of the Act was the raising of the school-leaving age, which ensured, as he saw it, that the effects of RE would be more permanent.

So the bill was passed with its new arrangement for church schools and its clauses making religious instruction and daily worship compulsory in all county and voluntary schools. The bill also laid down in some detail the methods by which a local education authority could draw up a new agreed syllabus, or adopt that in use in another area. This meant, in practice, that the consensus theology was to continue, with agreed syllabuses being drawn up by representatives of the churches in consultation with teachers and educationists. Winston Churchill was astonished when he discovered the method of planning the agreed syllabus and referred to the content of RE in county schools as the 'county council creed'. Temple seemed to have doubts about its positively Christian content and saw it as a kind of 'social ethicism' which nevertheless laid down a useful basis for a deeper appreciation of the Christian faith.

It was clear, however, that the Act intended the schools to produce Christians. Otherwise there would have been no need for the withdrawal clause which gives parents the right to remove their children from religious instruction or from school assembly.

We are so used to religious instruction and school assembly as elements of the school timetable that we are not always aware of how odd they are. In most other countries religious instruction is not laid down by statute, nor do children participate in daily worship as a fulfilment of the law of the land.

In the USA the first amendment to the constitution guarantees a 'wall of separation between church and state'. In practice this means that religious education is forbidden in state schools and there is no corporate act of worship. Such an act would be felt to compromise the strict neutrality of the state towards religion. The purpose of this neutrality is not, of course, to discourage religion, but to ensure freedom of belief and toleration between religions. It is perfectly possible for Catholic, Protestant, Mormon or Jewish communities to have their own private schools and to teach religion in them. But these must be privately financed. This caused a controversy recently, when some Roman Catholic educational institutions considered asking for government aid. It was made clear that if they had done so it would have meant forfeiting the right to teach religion.

In Australia and New Zealand there is no school-organized RE. Local ministers, however, are allowed to visit schools and teach those who belong to their own flock inside school hours.

In Japan, where there is a mixed religious heritage, there is a ban on religious education in state schools. But even in private schools there is caution. The most fiercely evangelical of the new Buddhist sects to have emerged in Japan since the war, the Soka Gakkai, has its own high schools for boys and girls and its own university. The Soka Gakkai believe in passing on Buddhist values in their schools. Their avowed aim is to create citizens for the twenty-first century who are capable of carrying on the human revolution initiated by the teachings of Saint Nichiren. Yet there is no form of religious instruction or worship, and children of parents who do not belong to the sect are under no pressure to convert.

In some of the new African countries religion is taught as part of the 'cultural heritage'. In Kenya it is considered important for children to know about traditional religion as well as about Christianity and Islam. There are of course many Christian schools founded by missionaries, some of which offer a more denominationally-based approach. But in a country of mixed religions it is felt important that all the traditions should be taught in schools.

Western Europe offers a more complex situation. In Sweden there is a neutral approach to religion. It is taught in schools in such a way as to require no withdrawal clause. Denmark and Norway are stricter, and there is more control by the established church than there is in England. In Spain the Roman Catholic faith is taught in all state schools. In France, where there has been a long struggle over education between church and state, the neutral approach is adopted in schools.

It is only in England that the law requires religious education to be evangelical, but not church-based, linked to formal worship, but worship of no known denomination or sect.

Laws express policy but they cannot guarantee success. There follows a fictional commentary.

September 1955

The athletic young man arrived at Bridport House to discuss his duties with the headmaster before the beginning of term. The headmaster was delighted to have an Oxford half-blue on the staff. He greeted him warmly and launched into a discussion of the previous term's cricket results. The young man asked about rugger fixtures for the term ahead. The headmaster was just about to summon his wife to show the young man to his room when he suddenly remembered something. 'By the way,' he said, 'you won't mind helping out with Divinity, will you?' 'Divinity?' Faint dismay passed over the young man's face. He smiled quickly. 'We all do a bit,' the headmaster went on, 'it's compulsory for Common Entrance as you probably know. It's all fairly straightforward. Bit of the Bible, English Hymnal, and I think they ought to know the creeds by the time they leave.'

'I'd better mug them up, then,' said the young man, 'I'm . . . er . . . not much of a churchgoer myself . . .'

'Fine, fine,' said the headmaster, dismissing the subject. He rang the bell for his wife . . .

Sister Bridget Mary had just finished her class on the Reformation. The top form of eleven year olds at St Ignatius Roman Catholic Junior School had just learnt how the English heresy had originated in Henry VIII's insatiable desire for a series of new wives. Now she was off to Catechism class with the first form. She decided to speak to them about grace: 'A supernatural gift of God, freely bestowed upon us for our salvation.' The first form did not know their catechism yet, though it was never too early to start. Even at that age it was essential to lay the foundations of the Catholic faith, the foundation that would carry them through the storms and troubles of life. Once a Catholic always a Catholic. Secure in that conviction Sister Bridget Mary swept into the classroom and led the class in a resounding 'Hail Mary' . . .

Miss Irene Potter taught Scripture at Sunnyside Girls' Modern School. It did not agree with her, she wanted to be a missionary. Running the Girls' Friendly Society and teaching in her local school was a poor substitute for trekking around African villages with a Bible and a manual on agriculture. When she had started teaching a number of girls had come to the Lord and she had formed them into a prayer group which met after school. The headmistress, a middle-of-the-road Anglican, had heard about it and discouraged it. In this the headmistress was at one with the terrifying science mistress who openly poured scorn on the teaching of God's word. Miss Potter stayed at Sunnyside for nine years. It did not agree with her, but she knew the test of her faith was to carry on in adverse circumstances . . .

Across the road, Roger Short, headmaster of Sunnyside Boys' Modern and Technical, was preparing the term's assemblies. He was an agnostic and took firm charge of assembly to prevent it falling into the hands of enthusiasts. He was not opposed to religion, and felt, in his secret heart, that it might do the rowdy fourth year some good to undergo some lengthy devotion each morning. As it was he read every morning from Ecclesiastes and St Luke, occasionally adding an episode from *Pilgrim's Progress*, which he admired for its stern moral tone. There were five hymns in *Songs of Praise* that he approved of, and he led the school in the Lord's Prayer because it was something everyone ought to know . . .

NOTES

1. *The Fourth 'R'*: the Durham Report on Religious Education, SPCK 1970, p. 56
2. See *Return: School Board Schools*, Religious Teaching (Denbeigh), House of Commons, 1879, Circular 172. Quoted in *School Worship – an Obituary*: John Hull, SCMP 1975
3. *The Fourth 'R'*: p. 7
4. *School Worship – An Obituary*, p. 13
5. *Robert Gregory*: W. H. Hutton, Longmans 1912, p. 296. Quoted in *The Fourth 'R'*, p. 31-32
6. Tract written in 1918. Quoted, according to *The Fourth 'R'*, p. 37, in *Britain in the Century of Total War*: A. Marwick, Bodley Head 1968, p. 112
7. *The Winchester Syllabus of Religious Instruction*: new ed., 1921. Quoted in *School Worship*, p. 15
8. *The Cambridgeshire Syllabus of Religious Teaching for Schools*, 1924, p. VI. Quoted in *School Worship*, p. 17
9. Ibid. Quoted in *School Worship – an Obituary*, p. 19
10. See discussion in *School Worship – an Obituary*, p. 18 ff.

The original phrase is from John Hubbard, Anglican and MP, in 1865

11. *The Art of the Possible*: R. A. Butler
12. *The Idea of a Christian Society*: T. S. Eliot, Faber & Faber 1939, p. 21
13. Ibid. p. 23
14. Ibid. p. 24
15. Ibid. p. 34
16. Ibid. p. 37
17. Ibid. p. 64
18. White paper on *Educational Reconstruction*, 1943
19. 'William Temple as Thinker': W. R. Matthews. Essay in *William Temple: an Estimate and an Appreciation*, James Clarke & Co. Ltd 1946, p. 9
20. Broadcast, 10 February 1930
21. *Christus Veritas*: William Temple, p. 88
22. Speech to National Society in 1942 quoted in *William Temple – Archbishop of Canterbury*: F. A. Ironmonger, Oxford University Press 1948, p. 571
23. Opening Speech at first diocesan conference at Canterbury, July 1942. Quoted in *William Temple – Archbishop of Canterbury*, p. 571

CHAPTER TWO

God on the Timetable

The religious clauses of the 1944 Act were warmly welcomed by most of those who were responsible for the teaching of religion in schools: 'I believe that we ought to regard the Act as a great victory for Christian principles – a sure and certain proof that the work of the churches has not been such a failure as many people represent it to be.'[1] A leading secularist who had opposed the bill thought the act signalled a different kind of 'victory' for the church. By pressing for compulsory instruction in religion and worship the churches were: 'Announcing that they have exhausted their religious vitality and desire to be no more than an arm of the state's police power.'[2] But the educational principles laid down in the Act thoroughly justified the importance given to RE: 'It shall be the duty of the local education authority for every area, so far as their powers extend, to contribute towards the spiritual, moral, mental and physical development of the community by securing that efficient education . . . shall be available to meet the needs of the population of that area.[3] So one of the basic aims of the school was to promote the spiritual development of the community. RE and assembly were to set the tone for the life of the school. The 1944 Act also laid down the procedure by which a local education authority might change its RE syllabus. The local authority must convene a conference consisting of representatives from the Church of England, other religious denominations, teachers, and the authority itself. It is the task of the conference to come to unanimous agreement on the form of instruction to be given.

The agreed syllabus is, of course, a policy document. It represents the consensus of clergy, teachers and educational administrators in a particular area. It is important insofar as it reveals what 'official' policy is. But, when considering the syllabuses, it is important to remember as well that they are *only* policy documents, and they do not necessarily reflect what was actually taught in the classroom. It is quite likely that, even today, some RE teachers have never studied the syllabus which they are meant to be teaching, and would not know how to find a copy of the agreed syllabus even if they wanted to.

The syllabuses of following years, as one might expect, reflect the policy of the 1944 Act. It is typical of their creators to assume that the aim of RE is to lead the children into conscious relationship with God.

The West Riding Syllabus of 1937 was adopted in many other areas, and continued to be influential long after 1944. Its syllabus for infants begins with a section : 'On helping children to pray.' This is followed by instruction on 'nature-work' : 'By using a child's natural appreciation of life and beauty we keep alive the wonder which is the basis of reverence.' 'Nature work' is followed by advice to teachers on telling stories from the Bible. Finally, there is a section called 'expression activities' which is aimed at involving the children in service to the community : 'Beautifully arranged flowers can be taken to children absent through sickness, or can be sent to hospitals. The children may also be encouraged to help the hospitals and other children by making toys and by sending to them toys, clothes, books, or even eggs and fruit. The care of animals, already mentioned in the section on nature-work, is also a training in service.'[4]

The syllabus for juniors (8-11) was firmly based on the Bible. It begins with a section on the life of Jesus taken from the gospels under the title, 'The Hero of Heroes'. The approach is straightforwardly biographical, and suggests passages to be learnt by heart. The second section is based on the Old Testament, 'Heroes of the Hebrew story'; it starts with Abraham and ends with Daniel. The last section, 'Heroes of the Christian Church', is a study of the Acts of the Apostles, with further sub-sections on saints and missionaries.

The syllabus reveals some sensitivity to the problems of teaching the Old Testament: 'That the ideas of God and goodness found in the Old Testament narratives often fall short of the revelation of Jesus and are at times directly contradictory to it, must be honestly faced by the teacher, who will then remain fearless before the questions of a thoughtful child. "We do not think God is like that since Jesus has come", – "We should call that cruel and unfair today", – "Jesus would not have done that," – such phrases may occur not infrequently in Old Testament lessons when the heroes of old time are compared to the Hero of Heroes himself.'[5]

The syllabus for senior pupils was set in the context of their total schooling: 'The main task of a senior school will be to deepen happiness, to strengthen knowledge, to increase understanding, to encourage thoughtfulness, and to inspire the pupils with Christian views of life and conduct joined with a trust in God which will enable them to face life's problems and difficulties with courage and hope.'[6]

The RE syllabus for seniors undertook to ensure that the pupils knew something about modern Biblical research into the Old and New Testament texts, the Christian church in the modern world, and the relationship between science and religion. These three areas are of great importance. They raise issues about the historic accuracy of the texts, which until this stage has been taken for granted. They also raise the problems of the cultural setting of early Christianity, and the relation of Christianity to other cultures. The last area tries to make sense of religion in the light of the insights of Freud, Marx and Darwin. At the senior level, then, pupils were expected to come to

grips with some of the major problems of Christianity in
this century. Yet it's not clear how 'objective' the teacher
was meant to be in raising these issues. Elsewhere the
syllabus assumes that the Old Testament should be taught
as the progressive revelation of God, culminating in the
promise of the Messiah. Yet to assume this is to see the
Old Testament as a document of the faith of the Christian
church. It *is* that, but it is also scripture for the Jewish
community, who understand it in quite different terms.
Imagine how a Jewish child might feel about the interpretation presented in the syllabus being taken for
granted! It is so woven into the presentation of the
material that text and interpretation have almost become
indistinguishable from each other. The compilers of the
syllabus were aware of current critical work on the Old
Testament text, and, for the teachers' benefit, they spelt
out the four sources theory of the Pentateuch, which
goes back to the German scholar Wellhausen. But there
is no real attempt to link this critical study to the pupils'
appreciation of the text as a whole.

In the section on the New Testament which follows
there are, again, some concessions to modern scholarship.
Yet the aim is still to present pupils with a biography of
Jesus drawn from the four gospels and supplemented by
other New Testament material. A third section examines
the development of the early church, a fourth maps out
a history of the church from the apostolic age to the
Oxford Movement, leaving out the entire history of the
Eastern Orthodox churches and the Roman Catholic
churches after the reformation. 'Christianity Today',
which follows, is a survey of missionary work and Christ-
ian-inspired philanthropy. The final section, on science
and religion, is to be left for the last year, and is only to
be tackled by those who are thought capable of it. The
aim is to show that there is no fundamental opposition
between science and religion. They are different paths to
the same truth, and both are necessary. Science is to be

regarded as a servant of mankind, and it needs the guiding principles of ethics and religion.

How should we assess a syllabus like this? There are two important aspects to the answer. First, the syllabus reflects the view that education requires the assimilation of a body of knowledge. The courses throughout are Bible-based. Whatever the 'religious' aims of the syllabus, they will only be achieved inasmuch as the pupil learns and assimilates the material presented to him. This does not exclude experiment, and experience, as we see from the section on teaching infants. But the main aim is to enable the pupil to wrestle with and absorb the body of knowledge contained in the syllabus. According to this view the pupil is rather like an empty vessel waiting to be filled with facts, information and values. Secondly, the knowledge acquired incorporates values. Text and inter- pretation go together. The stories from the Bible are to be presented in such a way as to induce a Christian response. This method of teaching and the way of im- parting values which it implies was, until quite recently, taken for granted. Even Plato, in *The Republic* would have approved: 'The beginning, as you know, is always the most important part, especially in dealing with any- thing young and tender. That is the time when the character is being moulded and easily takes any impress one may wish to stamp on it.'[7] The pupil here is like clay to be moulded into shape by the teacher: 'Our first business will be to supervise the making of fables and legends, rejecting all which are unsatisfactory; and we shall induce nurses and mothers to tell their children only those which we have approved . . .' 'We have now dis- tinguished the kinds of stories that may and may not be told about gods, demigods, heroes and the world below. There remains the literature concerned with human life . . .'[8]

Plato would have found little to quarrel with in the methods adopted by West Riding in 1933. Yet this

approach does raise problems today. In religious teaching
the relationship between the Bible and its Christian interpretation is no longer self-evident – except inside the
Christian churches. The same problem of event and interpretation can be seen if we look at the teaching of another subject, history. Many will remember using history
text books which presented the expansion of the British
Empire as the climax of world history and civilization.
H. E. Marshall's *Our Island Story*, for instance, presents
itself as a popular history for children. In fact, it is an
amazing confusion of myth, fairy tale, 'factual' description
and preaching. It begins with the myth of Neptune presenting his favourite son, Albion, with the island of
Samothea, which rose 'like a beautiful gem in the blue
water'. The island was called Albion at first. Later, Brutus,
Prince of Troy, conquered the native giants and made his
home there. 'Although after this the little island was no
longer called Albion, Neptune still loved it. When he grew
old and had no more strength to rule, he gave his sceptre
to the islands called Britannia, for we know, "Britannia
rules the waves".'[9]

This approach to history is not very far away from the
parody of *1066 and All That*, which is dedicated in the
'compulsory preface' to 'the great British people without
whose self-sacrificing determination to become top nation
there would have been no (memorable) history. History
is now at an end . . . this history is therefore final.'![10]

Now while it's true that neither of these books would
have been regarded as 'serious' history to be examined
at examination level, yet all history teaching involves the
problems of fact and interpretation. A traditional Roman
Catholic school could teach the history of the English
Reformation as if it was merely an offshoot of Henry the
Eighth's lust for a new wife. A Protestant or agnostic
history teacher might present it as a very positive step
away from subordination to Rome which has had
thoroughly beneficial effects. Both teachers are dealing

with the same facts, and yet those facts are not 'bare' facts, they are presented as the teacher interprets them, whether he does this consciously or unconsciously. The problem with *Our Island Story* is that we no longer share its conclusion. We do not know what 'stories' in Plato's sense to tell our children about our past that will make sense of our present.

But the RE of the West Riding Syllabus was a fully conscious attempt to make children Christians. It did not recognize that there is a distinction to be made between facts and interpretation. There was nothing unusual about this, given the climate of the time, in which it was considered appropriate to mould all children for their role as citizens of Christendom. No one, with the possible exception of the secularists, questioned the concept of Christendom – that alliance of the churches with the values of liberal democracy which laid the foundations of the 1944 Act.

There were, however, questionings about educational method. These started in the 1960s with the discoveries of the educationist Piaget, who devoted himself to the study of how young children learn. He outlined three stages in the development of the child's learning ability. Between the ages of four and seven the child's responses were intuitive, from eight to eleven the child became able to think in concrete terms, and from eleven upwards the development of abstract thought began. Piaget was applying psychology to education, and his work has had a lasting effect on educational theory, particularly as it applies to younger children. Perhaps the enthusiasm with which this 'child-centred' approach was received can be traced to the breakdown of historical and religious certainties. If the teachers no longer knew what to teach, let the children create their own timetables! Syllabuses had to be geared to what children could realistically cope with. Learning was to be natural – an extension of the child's natural curiosity. Many new primary schools aban-

doned the divisions between classrooms, and the pattern
of desks in straight rows. The school day was no longer
divided into rigid 'subject' areas. Children were encouraged
to learn by experience. Rote learning of tables and
languages was definitely out. So was the philosophy of
competition. Every child should develop at his own pace
and there could be no losers. The new methods were much
more demanding for teachers and parents. They involved
more in the way of personal skills at forming relationships
and giving sympathy than the old methods had done. It
was far more taxing to act as a 'resource person' for a
child doing a project, than it was to drill him in tables.

Changes in method went hand in hand with changes in
educational philosophy. The first of these was the widespread idea that all children were inherently educable.
Misunderstanding the Latin root of the word 'education'
people frequently claimed that 'to educate' meant 'to
draw out' (e-ducere), in other words, to draw out the
inherent potential of each child. In fact there is a Latin
verb 'educare', which is the real root of 'educate', and
means 'to train'. But the myth was widespread and led
to some starry-eyed idealism. Leila Berg writes in *Risinghill: The Death of a Comprehensive School*: 'Risinghill
children can express themselves. They have become used
to reasoning things out. They did not arrive at the school
like this. This was quite a deliberate education they
received at Risinghill. It was deliberate not in the sense
that it took place only at certain times and in certain
rooms, for it had often been quite spontaneous, but in
the sense that the discussion was instigated by people
who thought that what these children were thinking and
feeling was important, and it was education not in the
sense of conditioning, of controlling the child's conclusions, but in the true sense of *drawing out* the child's
potentialities that were already there.'[11]

This kind of thinking drives a wedge between the

experiential aspect of learning and the factual, informative side. It assumes that the facts will be absorbed *through* experience, and suggests that the old methods hindered the child from genuine experience by overloading him with facts that were outside his experience.

When this philosophy is interpreted in the context of religious education it leads to an important change of approach. For example, in many Roman Catholic schools the basic form of religious instruction was through the question and answer method of the catechism. Even the very youngest children were taught the essentials of the faith by repetition. The idea was, presumably, that even if they did not understand the concepts they were learning about, the ideas would become fixed in the mind in verbal form, and would provide a solid foundation for a more mature understanding. Often, however, it did not work out like that. When educational psychologists influenced by Piaget came to look at this method of teaching, they reported the grave dangers of trying to instill abstract concepts in children who were only able to think in the concrete. In the catechism, for example, children were introduced to words like 'soul' and 'grace'. They tried to find mental pictures for these ideas, and came up with concrete images. Many children pictured the soul as a kind of white disc somewhere inside the body. When they were told that sin blackened the soul, or caused black marks to appear in the soul, the image was reinforced, as it was again by the idea that baptism washes the soul white again. 'Grace' for many was a kind of white or golden liquid – something that is 'poured in'. The problem with these pictures is that it is very difficult for most children to move beyond them once the images are fixed. There are still many adults who inevitably 'see' grace and sin in concrete terms. Some reject religion because they find the picture-language absurd, others struggle on, hindered by their incapacity to break free from the images.[12]

As far as teaching method went, then, Piaget had an
important effect on some aspects of RE teaching, especially on the teaching of young children. But the child-
centred philosophy of education had a deeper impact on
RE. The West Riding syllabus had clearly been *subject*-
centred – it had aimed to impart a body of knowledge. In
1961 Harold Loukes brought out a survey on the effectiveness of RE. *Teenage Religion* revealed a bewildering lack
of knowledge about the Bible and utter confusion over
issues of doctrine. He reported, however, that there was
a deep interest among secondary school children in
religious and moral issues. His method was in line with
the child-centred, psychological approach. He was concerned that the children who took part in the survey
should speak freely and with candour. In some schools
he arranged for a class discussion to be tape-recorded, in
others he invited children to listen to the tape-recordings
and make written comments. He did not use statistical
methods. He was not interested so much in what proportion of adolescents believed in God, or what Bible
stories they remembered, but with how far religion helped
them to make sense of the human condition and of their
own adolescent situation. The motives which lay behind
the survey were *pastoral*. Harold Loukes was concerned,
not with how many *facts* about religion the children had
absorbed, but how *relevant* religion was to their own
lives. His attitude is that of a priest to his flock – he is
concerned with the condition of their souls. As a result
of his investigations, he developed the idea of 'Problem-
centred RE'. This is, of course, an extension into RE of
the child-centred approach which some educationists were
advocating for all subjects. But it still involves a special
place for RE and a special significance for it in the life of
the school. The RE class is the place where the adolescent
is encouraged to make sense of himself, it is a place where
he can discuss his own doubts and fears, hopes and
problems. The 'problem-centred' approach means that

ordinary questions of identity and meaning are considered in the light of Christianity. But the theology was to be kept hidden. It formed the vital undercurrent of meanings, but it was not necessarily to be brought to the surface in the classroom: 'Merely to ask the question, "Did God create the world?" is to push out horizons, for it raises at once the other question, "Or did the world just happen?" To ask "Is Jesus divine, and does he represent an intention of God for humanity?" is to raise the other question, "Or may man be just what he pleases?" And to consider the doctrine of the Holy Spirit is to ask, "In the apparent hopelessness of the human predicament is there really hope or is there really no hope?" '[13]

Harold Loukes considered that a change of role was required of the RE teacher. He was no longer to be an evangelist or instructor of the faith: 'Instead of netting his fish he must tackle them and hope they will swim in the right direction.' He does not question the assumption that problems of identity and meaning are really questions which can *only* be answered by the Christian faith, but he was not alone in this assumption. The re-application of Christian doctrines to questions of human meaning was not only going on in the schools. To understand the broader dimensions of problem-centred RE we must consider the theology of the sixties. This began with a tentative collection of essays, *Soundings*, by a group of theologians who considered themselves to be on the radical wing of the church. It exploded with the publication of Bishop John Robinson's *Honest to God*. It went through the weird intensities of the Death of God movement, and the glorification of the secular city by American theologians Paul van Buren and Harvey Cox, and it ended with the strange resurrection of *Godspell*, in which the dead Jesus was carried off the stage to a rousing chorus of 'Long Live God'.

The sixties were a difficult time for religion. It was the time of the greatest confidence that science and technology

would build a better human society within recent
history. The other side of that confidence was the terror
of the bomb, to which the Easter Aldermaston marches
bore witness. 'Scientific' categories of thought were the
norm, and aspects of experience which did not fit them
became eccentric and embarrassing. John Robinson writes
of this embarrassment in *Honest to God*. It was not that
he no longer believed in God, or wanted to stop practising
Christianity, it was just that the traditional 'supernaturalist' categories in which the faith had been expressed no
longer seemed adequate. So he attacked the idea that God
was 'out there', and criticized the spatial language which
seemed to be implicit in the doctrines of the Incarnation
and the Ascension. What Bishop Robinson was really
attacking was the fixing of religious ideas in concrete
images – it is the problem of the old catechism come home
to roost. Current interpretations of religious language
were poor and narrow, and they rarely wrestled with the
central difficulty of Christian religion – how the maps of
dogma, rite and scripture fit the territory of authentic
experience. Poets did not stop writing poetry in the
sixties, but God-language had become a peculiar problem.

The way John Robinson agonized towards a different
approach to Christian belief is important for this era of
RE. In trying to reinterpret 'God' Robinson took his inspiration from the American theologian Paul Tillich,
whose life-long passion had been to find a meeting ground
between theology and secular culture. He had spoken of
God not as the transcendent creator of the beginning of
Genesis, but as 'the ground of being'. There was justification for this: Christian theology spoke of God as transcendent *and* immanent. The emphasis in the formal
worship of the churches was on his transcendence, which
could be pictured in religious art and described in liturgy
and hymns. In a scientific culture the transcendence of
God was more difficult to conceive; the notion became a
stumbling block. But perhaps it was possible to recover

God in his immanence, in the depth of human experience and relationships. At least, this was what John Robinson tried to do: 'We must start the other way round. God is, by definition, ultimate reality, and one cannot argue whether ultimate reality exists. One can only ask what it is like – whether, for instance, what lies at the heart of things and governs their working is to be described in personal or impersonal categories.'[14]

There were other problems over the person of Christ. For just as it was embarrassing to speak of God in terms of his transcendence, so the supernaturalist interpretation of Christ, as the pre-existent Son of God, became fraught with problems. John Robinson is one in a line of thinkers who have found that traditional language used to describe the divinity of Christ gets in the way of his real humanity. His answer to this problem seems rather orthodox now, in the light of more recent controversy, but at the time it was startling. For he presented a Christ 'from below'. Using a phrase of the martyr-theologian Dietrich Bonhoeffer, Robinson describes Christ as 'the man for others', the man who, in his sheer humanity, revealed God. The question which haunted him in *Honest to God* was: 'Who is Christ for us today?' The human Jesus who revealed the love of God in human terms was more approachable, and credible, than the divine saviour who 'came down from heaven'. Though this new approach shocked many people, it was utterly orthodox in that 'revelation' was rooted firmly in the personality of Christ. Hence: 'The life of God, the ultimate Word of God in which all things cohere, is bodied forth completely, unconditionally and without reserve in the life of a man – the man for others and the man for God.'[15]

John Robinson also developed Bonhoeffer's notion of 'religionless' Christianity. No one is very sure what Bonhoeffer meant by 'religionless' Christianity, or by his description of modern man as 'man come of age'. But in a scientific culture Robinson took it to mean that Christian-

ity could only survive and be relevant if it came to be
defined in *contrast* to religion. Religion belonged to the
age of immaturity. Jesus could only be saviour and Lord
of a secular age if he was realized as a thoroughly secular
man. At the end of his book John Robinson quoted from
Herbert Butterfield: 'Hold to Christ and for the rest be
totally uncommitted.'[16] There was little place in the new
Christianity for traditional forms of prayer or worship.
Robinson hinted at a new kind of spirituality, a 'holy
worldliness' in which the way to holiness led through
the world of action.

The theology of the sixties was fond of making distinc-
tions between Christianity and religion. John Robinson
explains the distinction by describing the difference between a 'Christian' film, and a 'religious' film. The two
should not be equated. A Christian film is one that
expresses Christian meanings and values. A religious film
on the other hand is a film about 'a certain area of
experience or activity'. Robinson suggests that a 'religious'
film could have a Biblical theme, it might be about Lourdes
or be set in a convent. The 'Christian' film may have
nothing to do with religion at all.

On this definition the television quasi-documentary
Cathy Come Home (1966) could be taken as a 'Christian'
film. It was about the plight of a homeless family, and
the heartlessness of modern bureaucracy. It was not the
explicit intention of writer and producer to make a
'Christian' film, but it was 'recognized' as a film which
made Christian judgements. On the other hand *Dirty
Habits*, a film based on Muriel Sparks's satirical novel *The
Abbess of Crewe*, has a 'religious' theme, but is actually
about political intrigue. The multi-million dollar Biblical
epics are 'romantic', they use religious themes to create a
visual spectacle, but they can in no way be described as
'Christian'.

The motive behind this separation of Christianity from
religion was credibility. Thoughtful Christians could see

that the churches were well on their way to becoming merely a group of sects. If religion was no longer credible in a scientific culture, could Christianity survive without religion? They were concerned to salvage what they could from the apparent collapse of religion in order to keep the dialogue with the world going. Perhaps we are too close to them in time to judge how successful they were. Their work could be seen as a skilful and timely piece of apologetic; on the other hand, it could be seen as a sell-out on the part of theologians and church leaders, a desperate attempt to maintain credibility at any cost.

The movement had important offshoots. One of these was the 'psychologizing' of Christian experience. This took its impetus from the language of God as 'the ground of Being'. If God is the ground of being, then he must be the ground of *my* being as an individual. Getting to know God must mean going inwards. Getting to know God will involve, and affect, other human relationships. If we cannot communicate with a transcendent God, we can still experience the ground of being in the encounters with other people which happen to us continually. If we believe the ground of being to be personal and unconditional love, then we 'realize God' – we are saved – in those relationships where we give ourselves in unconditional love to each other. This was a theme hinted at in Father Harry Williams's essay in the collection *Soundings*, which tackled the relationship between theology and self-awareness. Later, in a collection of sermons, *The True Wilderness,* he showed how doctrine could be 'psychologized'. Once doctrine stopped being regarded as a fixed 'deposit' of formulas to be grasped by the intellect, it could be broken open to yield inner, personal meaning. Here, for example, is his re-interpretation of the doctrine of the Trinity: 'In the doctrine of the Trinity we have set before us an image in which the threat of non-being is met and overcome. The threat of being isolated is overcome because the one God is de-

scribed as being eternally in relation . . . where there is
relatedness there can be no aloneness. At the same time
the doctrine provides us with an image where the opposite
threat of absorption is met and vanquished. The persons
of the Godhead are forever distinct and unconfused.'[17]

The Trinity then is interpreted as a 'saving' image. It
points to the fact that we are saved from the threat of
non-being, non-being brought about either by isolation or
absorption. In this kind of writing theology becomes
'problem-centred'. Christian doctrines become symbols
through which we can interpret our human condition,
alienation, hope and restoration. We have here a peculiar
alliance between Christianity and existentialism. Existent-
ialist philosophy accepts the impossibility of metaphysics.
We cannot know 'what is the case' about existence, we
can only create truth for ourselves by commitment and
action. Christian existentialism veers away from questions
about God – the questions whether, and in what sense
he can be said to 'exist' – and is suspicious of any
authority external to the self, whether of the church or
of the Bible. Christian truth is found in commitment and
involvement.

The effect of this theology on the teaching of religion
was indirect, but very important. RE had to be made
relevant. It had to start from where the children were.
If children were helped to explore honestly their sense
of wonder, fear, and doubt, they would discover the
'God-dimension' of life. Christianity was the key to self-
knowledge and self-understanding, for working out
relationships, for coming to terms with sex. Sex instruction, in some schools, became linked with RE. In Kidbrooke School a teacher in the RE department conducted
a series of lessons on sex and marriage as a regular part
of her syllabus. This met with the full agreement of the
science department on the grounds that 'the information
on reproduction in the science course should not be linked
with the human problems of marriage and family life'.

The course could well have included advice such as this, addressed to a class of girls: 'You are in some ways incomplete until you have found completion with the right man; not just sexual completion, but marriage. You and I, women, have a unique part to play in this matter as "helpmates" for man, as complements, partners.'[18] 'The adolescent wants religion to solve his personal problems for him' claimed Harold Loukes, meaning by 'religion' the Christianity of the agreed syllabus.[19] Problem-centred RE still made extraordinary and unique claims. It is 'the most important feature of school life',[20] because it provides resources for coping with the problems of adolescence. With non-adolescents the approach was experimental. In *Readiness for Religion* Ronald Goldman proposed that RE should be taught to young children through a series of 'life-themes'. The lesson should start from factors in the child's experience and lead up to a Bible story. So a project on the life of a shepherd led to the theme of Jesus as the Good Shepherd. A lesson which started by considering the properties of light led up to the description of Jesus as 'the light of the world'.

Even with older pupils it was assumed that 'problems' would lead to the Bible: 'The aim is to gain sufficient grasp of the grand argument that the specific problems of today can be set against the timeless statements of the Bible.'[21]

Like sixties theology, sixties RE was experiential, psychological and Jesus-centred. It tried to break away from using explicit theological or 'religious' language. It tried to present Christianity as distinct from religion, with its institutional, ritual and dogmatic aspects.

But in spite of the changes of emphasis and approach the task of RE was still different from that of other subjects on the timetable. RE was therapy for living in the heady and dangerous sixties: 'Our classes are aware that they are now entering a bewildering time: we must discover what it is that bewilders them, and face it, not as authorities who have all the answers, but as friends who stand by them as they grapple with their problems.'[22] It is interesting to compare that comment from Harold Loukes with the more measured and authoritarian tone of an agreed syllabus: 'We believe that the recrudescence of superstition, the prevalence of anxiety-neurosis, the wide-spread existence of the guilt complex and the un- certainty concerning moral values are all due to the absence of clear understanding as to why we should be- have as we are expected to. Only when the God who is both righteous and merciful is known again can any of these evils be overcome. A faith is essential for an inte- grated personality.'[23]

Some of the syllabuses reflect more explicitly the move- ment for child-centred education: 'The impetus for the writing of a new syllabus for Wiltshire came from what is described as research into the feelings and understanding of children about religion, and the various expressions of opinion about the needs of children for religion derived from these sources.'[24] While claiming to be non-icono- clastic, this syllabus continues with a careful explanation of the child-centred approach and its relevance for the teaching of religion. The compilers are aware that this could be misunderstood, and they are anxious to reassure those who might be tempted to interpret the new approach as a lapse into humanism. But they are clear that their aim is to make the subject less 'subject-centred' and more relevant to everyday life. Their suggestions include plans for work on 'Christianity in Wiltshire' which would involve visits to churches and sites of religious interest. The main aim of the syllabus is to equip the pupils to take part in the life of the church. They are to be helped in their journey from an immature to a mature under- standing of the faith. In that process they are to be encouraged to ask questions and raise doubts. The syllabus also has a more moral or humanistic aim; to help the children to learn responsible citizenship and to put into

practise the ideal of service. There was an additional aim
for the sixth form. They were to: 'Learn tolerance towards all men by some understanding of the beliefs, ways
of thinking and culture of non-Christians in this country
and in other parts of the world.'[25] Even rural Wiltshire
was aware by this time that one of the aims of RE in the
future would have to be a concern with the study of
other religions; but it is astonishing how long it was before
this was realized. After all there had been a significant
Jewish community in England for many years. There were
also the various sects, the Christian Scientists and the
spiritualists for example, which hardly fitted the mainstream tradition. There were also the children of humanist
parents. It was possible for parents to withdraw their
children from RE under the withdrawal clause. But in
industrial areas it was becoming less and less possible for
RE to go on as if the other religions did not exist. There
were growing numbers of immigrants from Asia (Hindus,
Sikhs and Muslims), the West Indies (Pentecostal Christian)
and from Greece, Cyprus and Turkey (Eastern Orthodox
and Muslim). There was also the quiet but numerous
Chinese community, some of whom were Christian and
some of whom held Buddhist or Taoist beliefs.

And yet the educationists were still suggesting: 'To
consider the doctrine of the Holy Spirit is to ask, "In the
apparent hopelessness of the human predicament is there
really hope or is there really no hope?" '[26] The questioner
seems to be unaware that a significant proportion of the
world's population might find hope in Mao or Marx, in
the militancy of the Islamic reform movements, or the
forced conversion of aggressive forms of Buddhism from
Japan. Religions other than Christianity had been ignored,
and the dichotomy between Christianity and religion
which was so useful to the theologians and apologists, in
fact hardened the impression that RE in the schools was
nothing more than an opportunity for evangelism on the
part of the established churches. Occasionally an agreed

syllabus gave the game away completely: 'The Syllabus is deliberately designed as. an evangelistic instrument, and the Christian should have no hesitation about using it as such . . . the subject to be taught is Biblical knowledge, not morality but the Christian faith, and the aim is to lead the pupils to a personal knowledge of Jesus Christ and to active life within a worshipping community. To achieve that purpose the Christian teacher may zealously use all his influence.'[27]

Of course, more liberal minded educationists would have disliked this blunt approach. But their own position reflected a fatal muddle. To return to the problem of 'belief in the Holy Spirit' – it is of course possible to *ascribe* all genuine forms of human hope to the Holy Spirit. This is a Christian understanding. But it is quite different to *equate* those forms of hope with the Church's belief in the Holy Spirit. What does a humanist make of being told that his compassion and concern for other men comes from the fact that he 'really' believes in the doctrine of the Holy Spirit? He probably feels he is being patronized, and he is. It may make sense in a Christian gathering to assume that the question of whether there is 'really hope or really not hope' is a question of the doctrine of the Spirit. In that situation the memories and nuances of Christian language are still reverberating in the group. But outside such a group the assertion has no substance.

It may be that teachers and educationists who welcomed the sixties approach were still assuming that the school was a Christian community and that Christian meanings *did* reverberate just below the surface. To many pupils, though, 'problem-centred' RE was simply incomprehensible. They suspected the evangelistic motive, but were bewildered by the fact that it was so often hidden. Something of this bewilderment is reflected in a recent survey of young people's beliefs carried out for the

Church of England's General Synod Board of Education. This shows the influence of the sixties approach to RE insofar as it still continues today. One boy who had left school some years previously recalls that RE was: 'A complete farce at my school . . . sometimes just a moral discussion on – *anything*'. Another, still at school at the time, replied: 'It's all current affairs. That girl who was attacked and in a six-day coma and she died. We talk about how they should be tried. We speak for what we believe in.' A third recalls a discussion in RE: 'It was a subject nothing to do with religion. It was sort of, you know, a period where you'd go in – it was called Religious Education. We could talk about football – talk about anything you want.' The researchers comment that: 'Many . . . enjoyed topical discussion – drugs, sex, capital punishment, etc. But they found it hard to accept this or even comparative religion as "really RE", or as particularly useful to them.'[28] Some teachers would support this conclusion. They see the failure of 'problem-centred RE' in the fact that so many children seemed to absorb so little from it. They do not know enough to have a real discussion, and are, to some extent, suspicious of the approach which is not overtly religious.

By the end of the sixties and the beginning of the seventies the concept of child-centred learning was under attack. It was apparent that educational standards were falling. More and more children were leaving school without having achieved even the most basic competence in the traditional 'three R's'. Linked to this was the increase in serious discipline problems in schools, particularly in the large inner-city comprehensives. Public alarm was expressed in television documentaries and in letters to the papers. Troubled commentators produced the 'Black Paper' collections of articles attacking the erosion of standards. There were calls to teachers to return to traditional teaching methods, to ensure at least that the majority of pupils were numerate and literate. 'A school is a place of learning rather than a temple of self-expression.'[29]

At the same time there was trouble at the other end of the academic world. The late sixties was the period of student revolt. Some saw this as the beginning of a Western cultural revolution. For others it was the culmination of a series of attacks on structured learning and the ideal of objectivity. David Martin, Professor of Sociology at the London School of Economics, experienced the long period of unrest at LSE which saw episodes of casual violence, the breakdown of academic discipline, and various acts of intimidation against the teaching community. With a son at a large and progressive comprehensive school, he found himself questioning much that had been taken for granted in previous years, in particular, the notion of experiential, pupil-centred learning: 'Self-determination emerges more easily when the person is gradually, clearly, overtly, firmly inducted into responsible roles, transferable rules, ordered relations. Learning by osmosis was intended to permit the intuition of general concepts, but in fact succeeds only in saturating the person helplessly in a *totally* particular context. A child intuiting a whole sentence is unable to read a single word . . .'[30] 'If nothing is passed on, if nothing is given, then nothing is received.'[31] His conclusion is not a total condemnation of progressive methods, but he considers that to rely on them alone is to court disaster. He quotes from a 'black paper' by Professor Bantock: 'Used competently these new methods have a great deal to offer. Used incompetently . . . they are probably more disastrous to learning than reliance on the old formal methods.'[32]

The choice between child-centred and subject-centred education, as Professor Martin sees it, is not a clear-cut either/or choice. What is necessary is a balance between fact and experience, between information and intuition. Both feed on each other in the growth towards maturity.

In another essay he explains how the churches, as well as the schools, are influenced by the fashion for innovation in such a way that the notion of handing down a living tradition from one generation to another has been undermined: 'Nothing is signified, but one seeks for the personally significant.'[33] For Professor Martin, education *is* induction into a society and a culture. The problem arising from this conclusion is to assess what sort of society and culture the next generation are going to be brought into. Is it a Christian society or a secular society? Is it a pluralist society with many different cultures living alongside each other? Or is it, in some sense, all these things at once on different levels?

In consideration of, and response to, these questions, the RE of the seventies has lurched off on a completely different direction. The agreed syllabuses of the late sixties and early seventies began to reflect this change.

The Inner London RE Agreed Syllabus for 1968 is a mixture of old and new. Its title is *Learning for Life*. From the introduction the aim seems fairly traditional: 'This syllabus is not only concerned with Christianity as an abstract concept, but with what it means in every age to be a Christian and to be religiously committed.[34] There follows a section on the techniques of teaching which firmly repudiates 'brainwashing' and 'indoctrination'. There is a place, though, for the 'reasoned teaching of Christian doctrine'.

The syllabus for the sixth form provides a detailed programme for the teaching of comparative religion: 'It is increasingly being realized that, in a syllabus on Religious Education, the study of non-Christian religions has a necessary place . . . It also becomes ever more obvious that in this country, and not least in London, we are living in a plural society, a society with a wide range of religious and cultural variety, and teachers have an obligation to take account of this, both as a matter of respect for the non-Christian pupils in the schools, and to help those in the Christian tradition to a sympathetic understanding of their fellow-pupils.'[35]

The compilers of this syllabus seem aware that what they are proposing is something of an innovation. They suggest that the starting point for teaching non-Christian religions is in the class itself – with the representatives of other religions who happen to be present. This is highly significant. Pupils of non-Christian parents might have been expected to withdraw their children from 'Christian' RE. And yet here it is suggested that they are to be a resource point for the teaching of the non-Christian religions. Clearly, then, the aim of the RE class is being conceived differently. But *Learning for Life* is not sure *how* differently. It ends with the rather lame conclusion that: 'Religion is a matter of practice as well as of theory. It will now be clear that this syllabus is concerned not only with Christianity as an object of theoretical study, but with what it means, in every sense, to be a Christian.'[36] There is nothing new in this. But earlier, in its introduction to the section on comparative religion, the syllabus considers the implications of the differences between the religious traditions. Discussion is bound to arise in the classroom and should be welcomed but: 'As members of the larger human brotherhood, all men, without reference to religion or race, should strive to promote justice and peace, goodwill and understanding among men and nations.'[37] The syllabus here is trying to justify the teaching of comparative religion on religious grounds by linking it to a universal ideal. It is a different ideal from the ideal which saw the RE class as a place of therapy. But it is still assuming that it is the purpose of the RE class to induce a religious response in the pupils. This is significant for two reasons. First, it is clear that the school no longer regards itself as a 'Christian' community. RE still claims to offer an opportunity 'to explore truth in its widest possible framework', but this is no longer an exclusively Christian framework. In the theology of the sixties Christianity was often presented as the truth beyond religion. Now we see a swing to the realization that religion is bigger than Christianity. Secondly, it seems that the syllabus intends to furnish the pupils with a religious attitude to life. Many would feel that this is not an objectionable aim. Yet it raises immediate problems. If the school is no longer a Christian community, what are the ideals by which it lives? There are hints in some of the newer syllabuses that Christianity has been replaced by a kind of pan-religious humanism, and the RE class is one of the places where this ideology is propagated. Other syllabuses, as we shall see, aim for a 'neutral' approach – an approach which separates fact from interpretation according to what is thought to be 'scientific method'. Both attempts tend to result in the kind of consensus which is produced by committees. It has little to do with the grass-roots communities which are represented in the school. It is still a consensus in which representatives of the Christian churches play a large part. It shows the extent to which educationists and clergy are still colluding in a kind of imperialistic mission to the schools. Recent debate on RE has revealed that collusion for what it is – a last-ditch attempt by the established churches to keep the schools inside Christendom – even at the cost of losing touch with historic Christianity altogether.

But lest we should imagine that educationists or clergymen are in any position to control what actually goes on in school, let us continue our fictional commentary:

June 1966

The young graduate crunched up the gravel drive in his blue denims and boots, his guitar swung over his back.

He found the head teacher brewing coffee in his room. There was no desk, but three large, comfortable chairs with brightly coloured cushions. Don (that was the head teacher's name) welcomed him, and pointed him to a chair. They sat down facing each other.

'I'm glad you didn't go through college,' said Don, 'they get you early in teacher training.'

'What do you see as my role here?' asked the young graduate. Don leant back and stirred his cup before replying: 'I think we're all explorers. Us and the kids, I mean. But it's not us and them. It's no good coming here with a structured timetable, expecting *results*.'

'All that's rather anti-life, isn't it?'

'Yuh, that's how I see it. When these kids leave here they've got to be rid of their parents' hang-ups. Sex, religion, middle-class values, you know the sort of thing. Get them to see the institutional church for what it is. When these kids leave here they've got to be . . .' he paused, looking for the right word in the depths of his coffee mug, 'REAL.'

Sunnyside, thought Roger Short, is getting over its teething troubles. No merger is easy, but we're getting through it. Of course, there'd been changes. Not everyone had liked them. Assembly had had to go, for example. There was nowhere they could have it, for a start. And it was divisive to hold separate ones in the old buildings. But there just wasn't room anywhere to have the whole school at once. He had the boys on their own sometimes of course. Told them some of the exciting things that he'd done during his national service. They liked that. He wished he could get rid of that awful scripture teacher. Why didn't she go off and be a missionary or something? She really was a relic. She believed in Adam and Eve, she'd *said* so in the staff room. Still, it was clear that she was making even less impression on the tough nuts of 4B than she'd made when she was only teaching girls. They're not stupid, these kids, thought Roger Short.

Sister Bridget Mary was worried. Anthea Sylvan-Stuart
had all the right credentials. She came from a good
Catholic family. Her brother was a priest. She went to
Mass every Sunday. She'd studied theology. The children
adored her. But whatever went on in her classes? Sister
Bridget Mary had been passing the classroom once, and
the door was open and they were singing a chorus, *not*
one she knew. And when she'd questioned three of the
first formers on some simple point from the catechism,
not one of them had known the answer! They won't be
able to recite the rosary next, she thought grimly. But
she was curious all the same. Whatever *did* Anthea Sylvan-
Stuart actually teach?

NOTES

1. *The School without the Parson*: E. F. Braley, REP 1945,
   p. 7 ff., as quoted in *School Worship*, p. 24
2. Remark attributed to Harold Laski. See *William Temple —
   Archbishop of Canterbury*, p. 577
3. *Education Act 1944*: ch. 31, part II, 7, HMSO
4. *Syllabus of Religious Instruction*: County Council of the
   West Riding of Yorkshire Education Department, February
   1937, pp. 6 and 7
5. Ibid.
6. Ibid. p. VIII
7. *The Republic of Plato*: translated by F. M. Cornford,
   Oxford 1941, p. 67
8. Ibid. pp. 66 and 67
9. *Our Island Story*: H. E. Marshall, Thomas Nelson & Sons
   Ltd, p. 3
10. *1066 and All That*: R. J. Yeatman and W. C. Sellar,
    Methuen & Co. Ltd 1930, pp. VII, VIII
11. *Risinghill — Death of a Comprehensive School*: Leila
    Berg, Pelican 1963, p. 219

12. 'The Roman Catholic children and what they are being taught': Derek Lance, in *Religious Education*, Darton Longman & Todd, p. 43

13. *Teenage Religion*: Harold Loukes, SCMP 1961, p. 96

14. *Honest to God*: J. A. T. Robinson, SCMP 1963, ch. 2, p. 29

15. Ibid. p. 77

16. *Christianity and History*: Herbert Butterfield, 1949, p. 146, as quoted in *Honest to God*

17. *The True Wilderness*: H. A. Williams, Constable & Co. Ltd 1965, Fontana 1976, p. 121f

18. From a first-hand account by Mrs Hills Cotterhill, then at Kidbrooke School. See *Teenage Religion*, appendix A, pp. 153-155

19. *Teenage Religion*: p. 103

20. *Agreed Syllabus of Religious Instruction*: County of Lincoln, parts of Lindsey Education Committee, 1964, p. 9

21. *Teenage Religion*: p. 151

22. Ibid. p. 145

23. See 20, p. 9

24. *Religious Education in Wiltshire*: Wiltshire County Council Education Committee, 1967, p. 3

25. Ibid. p. 102

26. See 12

27. *Agreed Syllabus – Lincoln*: p. 10

28. *Young People's Beliefs* – General Synod Board of Education Research Report: Bernice Martin and Ronald Pluck, 1976, p. 27

29. *Tracts Against the Times*: David Martin, Lutterworth Press 1973, p. 122

30. Ibid. p. 146

31. Ibid. p. 148

32. Ibid. p. 127

33. Ibid. p. 148

34. *Learning for Life*: the Agreed Syllabus of Religious Education of the Inner London Education Authority, 1968, introduction p. 9

35. Ibid. p. 85

36. Ibid. p. 90

37. Ibid. p. 86

CHAPTER THREE

God, Exams and Politics

RE has always been an academic subject. That is, it is possible to take state exams in it, and to relate it to higher academic courses in theology or religious studies at university level. Some schools which teach RE at 'O' and 'A' level, or for CSE, regard this as a separate activity from the weekly class which includes everyone. It is assumed that only a few will specialize in religion, and they will need a more serious and academic approach than is possible in the weekly session on morality, relationships or world religions. The exam syllabuses for 'O' and 'A' level and CSE do not presuppose a religious commitment on the part of the person taking them. The exams test knowledge and degree of understanding, as in any other subject. With some examination boards the range of options is wide. Even within the study of Christianity it is possible to study the Greek New Testament, forms of liturgy, the Reformation and basic questions of morality and ethics. Some boards have included options for Jewish children wishing to be examined in Hebrew. Others are introducing this principle more widely, so that a Hindu child, say, can get an 'O' or 'A' level pass in the study of his own religion. Sometimes RE has been regarded as an easy option at exam level, as has theology at university level. But in practice, as many have found, RE and theology are far from easy options. They are serious disciplines requiring a number of different skills and an open and critical mind. No one passes an RE exam because he is religious. It is not the purpose of an exam to test faith!

The fact that a subject can be examined suggests that

it is taken seriously as an academic subject. In the past
the agreed syllabuses have rather played down this aspect
of RE. This was because, of course, RE was regarded as
'too important' to be judged like a normal subject. It was
not concerned with academic questions but with life and
faith. Over and over again the syllabuses tell us that
Christianity is not just an academic subject, with the
implication that 'academic' subjects are rather inferior.
RE is concerned with the 'whole' person, unlike mathe-
matics or history. This downgrading of the academic side
of RE by scores of well meaning clergy and Christian
teachers is one of the main problems in the way of
recovery for RE. At the same time it seems rather unfair
to imply that those who teach other subjects are only
interested in exam results. All those who care about the
education of children are concerned with their wholeness
and growth of personality. There is no reason why this
should be the special prerogative of the RE class. Some-
body ought to ask why the science teacher who approved
of RE being extended to include sex education did not
feel that questions of human relationships came within
her brief.[1]

But from the point of view of RE the refusal to treat it
with any academic seriousness, and to separate the exam
teaching from the rest of it, means that for many children
it is a 'bogus' subject. It is preaching, masquerading as
education: 'RE don't get you on in the world unless you
want to be a vicar . . .' 'Religion's a sign you're not
educated . . .' 'I hated the whole thing. It was like being
made to eat something you didn't want to eat.'[2] One
teenager who took part in this survey was asked what
form he thought RE ought to take in schools: '. . . It
should be written work, things you can look at in a book
. . . they should give you homework in it . . . You could
give an exam in it, that sort of thing.' It was quite clear
to this interviewee that a subject was to be taken seriously
if it involved homework and exams, and if it didn't, then

it was a waste of time. Educationists may deplore this attitude, but in a world where so much store is set on examination results, it is perfectly understandable. The system of exam-centred education should perhaps be questioned. But as long as schools have some way of evaluating a pupil's progress in a subject, RE will only become credible insofar as it shares the same system of evaluation.

Yet it is clear that the public examination syllabuses are open minded in their approach to religious truth. They do not examine the degree of faith or commitment, or even the extent to which RE 'makes sense' to pupils. Why is their approach not adopted in the classroom, in the general RE class? Some religious people would argue that the academic approach sounds 'dry'. But there is no reason why it should be drier than any serious subject. The trouble is that RE has been a course in Christian initiation or a therapy class for real or imagined adolescent problems. It has been anything but a normal part of the school timetable. But religious educationists today are presenting new arguments for keeping RE on the school curriculum. These arguments are educational, not religious.

A Schools Council Project on RE in Primary Schools which was conducted by the University of Lancaster argues firmly that, without RE, education is incomplete. Religion has been, and still is, one of the most potent forces in the shaping of human society. Art, literature, history and geography are incomprehensible without some grasp of what religion is and what part it plays in shaping human culture. Religion is universal in that the questions it attempts to answer are universal questions, and not limited to those who find answers in a particular tradition. It is not the function of RE to initiate a child into one tradition, it is rather to give him an appreciation for, and a sympathy with those who hold religious beliefs and those who reject religion altogether : 'If we exclude learn-

ing about religion from the general pattern of learning,
we may suggest one of two things to the children: either
religion is so special that it has nothing to do with ordinary
human experience or it is so irrelevant to everyday life
that schools should not be concerned with it.'[3]

It is clear, however, that the different religions should
not be treated like the different Christian denominations.
There are different religions, but it is probably misleading
to assume there is such a thing as 'religion' of which they
are all expressions. But there are certain common questions which all the religions are concerned with. These
are listed as:

Why does anything exist at all?
Is there any purpose in existence?
Is man answerable for what he does with his life?
If so, to whom?
Should anything be regarded as sacred?
If so, why?
What value should be put on human life?
Why do the innocent suffer?
Is death the end?[4]

These are the fundamental questions of religion and the
answers to them differ. Some would reject the possibility
of ever finding an answer, but even so, the questions
remain: 'Every person adopts some cosmic view of things,
some faith or philosophy by which to live.'[5]

This may be what religion is, but put like this it
sounds both abstract and complex, a mind-stretching programme for adults, let alone children. In fact, the value
of asking questions like this is that it helps to map out
the area of human experience with which religion is
concerned. The Lancaster project puts forward the thesis
that religion is an area of human experience which, like
any other area, is open to study. The school is a good
place for beginning such a study, as it should provide an

open-ended, enquiring atmosphere. The study is not committed in advance to any degree of belief or non-belief. Whatever the presence of belief or non-belief at home, the child can be encouraged to an open-minded approach at school.

RE teaching is not only for explaining religion in terms of its effects on society and culture. A course should be designed to help the child to appreciate what it would be like to be religiously committed, though it is no part of the school's business to direct him towards any particular form of commitment. Still, the question of commitment is bound to arise, and an RE course should be one factor in helping children to make up their own minds about religion. The aim of RE becomes rather similar to the aim of a course on political science. Political science should help children to become politically aware, it should show them how to use their vote responsibly, but it cannot tell them *how* to use their vote. RE should make children religiously aware, but it cannot guide them into a faith.

If it is accepted that religious study is valid on educational grounds then there should be no problem in making it an important element in the school's curriculum. It may well be felt that one lesson a week is not nearly enough. It is at least as important a means to the understanding of human culture as history or geography. Advocates of the new RE do not always make this point, but it follows that if RE is to be seen alongside geography and history, then it should, like them, be regarded as a subject that can be dropped. If it is a serious examination subject it must be one that can be voluntarily chosen. This means, of course, that RE can no longer continue to be compulsory. The new RE should not need the protection of the 1944 Act. Nor does it need the withdrawal clause. Since it is no longer the purpose of RE to make children Christians (or anything else) no parent should have qualms about letting his children attend.

How do proponents of the new RE recommend that it

should be taught? Most teachers working with younger children will want to stay within the framework of Piaget, and base their courses on the different stages of the child's development. Like the old RE, the new approach starts from the young child's sense of wonder, mystery and imagination. As the child grows up he will acquire some awareness of religion as a fact of life. He will certainly be aware of Christmas, and possibly of Easter. He will see church buildings and may hear church services on radio or television. If he comes from a religious background he will himself have participated in worship. He may himself have tried to pray, or to have wondered what happens after death. If he is at a school where there are children of more than one faith he will be aware of the part religion plays in their lives. He will come to know that Muslim children go all day without eating during the month of Ramadan. He will have Sikh friends who wear turbans.

The new RE starts from these facts of life. It is child-centred in that it starts from what the child has seen, heard and felt. But its purpose now becomes informative. Religion, as the child observes it, is a phenomenon which needs explaining. Ninian Smart, who is one of the pioneers of the new RE, describes this approach as 'phenomenological'. In conveying information about religion, teachers should be aware of certain formal characteristics which are found in various degrees in all the religions. These are:

Doctrines, beliefs or official teachings.
Myths, beliefs and insights presented in story form.
Ethics, principles or codes of behaviour.
Rituals, public prayer and ceremony.
Experience, the faith of the individual believer.
Society, the community of faith produced by religion.[6]

If these six categories are valid for all religions then it can be said that religion involves beliefs about reality which go beyond what can be deduced by natural observation, and results in an individual and communal commitment to live in a certain way.

The first method for the new RE is observation. A teacher trying to convey what Christianity is about may be more likely to take children round a parish church, and show them the architecture, vestments, candles, crosses, prayer books and Bibles, than to sit them down with a book about the life of Jesus. In this way of teaching Christianity will not be protected from religion or presented as a truth beyond institutional religion. It will be seen *as* a religion, from the outside, as it were. The new RE tries to observe religion as it is, warts and all. It is far away from the old attempts to sell an idealized version of the Christian faith taken from the scriptures and interpreted through the liberal assumptions of committees of clergy and teachers.

The new approach has a lot in common with sociology. Sociology is usually presented as a science. It is the application of scientific method to the study of human society. Not all sociologists agree that sociology *is* really a science, but on the whole it appears to speak with the authority of the so-called natural sciences. The phenomenological approach to religion is in line with the scientific paradigm. Later we will consider whether the natural sciences do, in fact, offer the most appropriate model for the study of religion. Even if they do, it is clear that proponents of the new RE do not think that RE ends in sociology. It is here that a new muddle begins. For the educationists, in spite of their new approach, have inherited the conviction that RE is, in some sense, a special subject, different from all others. RE is the arena for moral questions, and for personal therapy. Moral questions which arise out of biology, physics or history are dealt with in RE. This will become obvious when we consider the new shape of the syllabus.

We should notice one important change that arises

from the new approach. Previously it was thought that the faith of the teacher was one of the most important factors in RE teaching. The new RE sees sympathy and enthusiasm as being infinitely more important. A hostile humanist and a bigoted fundamentalist will both teach the subject badly. But any competent teacher with the right degree of knowledge and sympathy should feel that RE is an option open to him. Not that it is an easy subject to teach. There is an immense amount of ground to cover in the study of religion, and the new RE is more, rather than less, intellectually demanding. But the personal convictions of the teacher are no longer the main qualification for teaching the subject.

The shape of the syllabus is the biggest unresolved problem so far. The list of religious questions suggested earlier might have seemed fairly all-inclusive. But what about non-religious responses to cosmic questions? What is the boundary of religion? Here we come up against a problem of English language. According to the Shorter Oxford English Dictionary religion is: 'Action or conduct indicating belief in, reverence for, and desire to please a divine ruling power . . . recognition on the part of man of some higher unseen power as having control of his destiny.' Under this definition some forms of Hinduism and most forms of Buddhism would be excluded. Buddhism began as a protest against the idea of a controlling God. The monastic Buddhism of South-East Asia, and the Zen school in Japan would not count as religion at all under this definition. The definition also excludes those movements which deny the existence of God and the after-life altogether, though there is some evidence that they may *function* rather like religions. Marxism and Humanism are real attempts to find an answer to, or a way of living with, the human dilemma. Should they be studied alongside religion, even though they are not included in the meaning of the word 'religion' as it is usually defined? Does it matter that humanists and Marxists have usually opposed religion as the embodiment of oppressive and anti-human forces?

These questions came to the surface in a fierce political battle over the revision of the Agreed Syllabus in Birmingham, which began in 1969. The previous syllabus had been drawn up in 1950, and was based on the Bible, aiming to impart to children an understanding of the Christian faith. The introduction to the new syllabus started by explaining that Birmingham society had changed a good deal since 1950. In twenty-five years Birmingham had become a multi-racial city. There was already a long-established Jewish community, now there were new immigrants from Asia and the West Indies. Muslims, Sikhs and Hindus came from India, Pakistan and Bangladesh. Pentecostal Christians and members of the Rastafarian cult came from the Caribbean. Race was a political issue, with large areas of the city being virtually taken over by the new communities. Naturally enough, the communities were trying to preserve their own identity in a strange land. To outsiders, this made the black areas look like ghettoes. The problems of education in these areas, were, and are, vast. In some families there was no one who spoke English. Children who went to English schools needed special help, which often was not available. Too many young people left school with almost no education and with dim prospects of getting a job. The compilers of the new RE syllabus were aware of these immediate social problems. In schools where sometimes over half the school came from non-English backgrounds the old Bible-based RE clearly would not do.

The new syllabus also pointed out in its introduction the changes that had been taking place in the educational philosophy of RE. It drew on the phenomenological approach which was already evolving, as we have seen, at Lancaster, inspired by Ninian Smart who had previously been a professor in the Department of Religious Studies at Birmingham University. His place at Birmingham was taken by John Hick, who specialized in the philosophy of religion, and had written on Christianity and the other world religions. Professor Hick became chairman of the co-ordinating working party of the conference called to revise the syllabus. The composition of the rest of the conference shows a significant departure from the past. The 1950 conference not only had no non-Christian representatives, it had no Roman Catholics either. The 1970 conference included a Roman Catholic, a Jew, a Muslim, a Sikh and a Hindu. Four other members were co-opted to serve on the various working parties set up by the conference. Among them was Dr H. Stopes-Roe, a leading member of the British Humanist Association.

In 1974, after four years of deliberation, the conference produced a new agreed syllabus. It was a slim volume, bound in green. At the same time, a very much more substantial handbook of suggestions for teachers was published in loose-leaf form under the title *Living Together*.

The syllabus declared that the subject of study from now on was not 'religion' so much as 'stances for living'. Humanism and Communism were part of the syllabus, and were to be studied in their own right, alongside the religions. As soon as it was realized that Birmingham Education Authority was proposing that Communism should be taught in the RE class there was a public outcry. Headlines in the papers shrieked of a Marxist plot. A politically conservative group on the education committee immediately protested. There was a public rebuke from the Bishop of Birmingham. In spite of this the education committee accepted the new syllabus in May 1974.

The problem was that the new syllabus was clearly illegal according to the terms of the 1944 Act. In no way could the study of Communism be regarded as fulfilling the requirement for religious instruction. Indeed, the whole notion of teaching 'life-stances' instead of 'religion' was a contradiction of the act, in letter and spirit. A Church of England group took the next step. The National

Society for the Promotion of Religious Education con-
sulted legal opinion on the issue. The society's advisors
assured them that the education committee was standing
on very shaky ground in accepting the new syllabus. On
the advice of the Department of Education and Science
the education authority hastily took steps to re-convene
the conference, and made it clear to the members that it
was their job to produce a syllabus that satisfied the
requirements of the law.

So, in 1975 a new version of the syllabus was produced.
This did not exclude the teaching of 'non-religious life-
stances', but it did mean they had to be related to the
teaching of religion, and not taught for their own sake.
They could be compared and contrasted with religion, but
not presented as equal alternatives. The syllabus was to be
about religion.

The change in emphasis can be seen by comparing the
two versions of the syllabus. A key passage in the 1974
version reads: 'The purpose of "Religious Education" is
not only to enlarge and deepen the understanding of the
different *stances for living* to which different people are
committed, but also, in some cases, to stimulate within
the pupils a personal search for meaning, and in others,
to illuminate the sense of meaning which they already
have.'[7] In the 1975 version the same passage becomes:
'The syllabus should be used to enlarge and deepen the
pupil's understanding of *religion* by studying *world
religions* . . . it should also stimulate the pupils and assist
them in the search for a personal sense of meaning in
life whilst enabling them to understand the beliefs and
commitments of others.'[8] The teachers' handbook *Living
Together* was also subject to revision, though it has continued to a large extent to embody the philosophy behind
the illegal syllabus. It is a large and thorough work, clearly
laid out, with detailed lists of books and class materials,
a most useful list of organizations offering help to RE
teachers, and a calendar of festivals and special events of

religious significance. *Living Together* adopts a self-consciously neutral stance: 'Religious education is concerned
with children as children, in the hope that they will
become thoughtful and tolerant adults with coherent
belief, and not as potential Christians, Muslims, Sikhs,
Humanists, etc.'[9]

Thus it is indicated that the aim of RE is to help
children appreciate what a religion, and a non-religion, is,
and to gain some insight into what it would be like to
be committed to a religion, or a non-religion. The handbook emphasizes the importance of an exploratory
approach, starting from the child's experience of wonder,
awe and love. There follow course outlines for children
from five to twelve on the major faiths: Christianity,
Judaism, Islam, Sikhism, Hinduism. In the original version
'The Secularist Way' appears as the last of these courses.
The course outlines for adolescents are divided into three
sections. Section one has two parts; the first looks at the
major religions, the second at Humanism and Communism. The second section is headed 'The Individual' and
concerns questions such as private morality, money,
friendship, sexuality, smoking and drugs, work and
leisure. The third section is headed 'The Community' and
considers, among other topics, the welfare state, the aged,
the sick, trades unions, the mass media, war and famine.
At sixth form level a course on Buddhism is outlined, and
the phenomenon of religion is to be considered under its
philosophical, comparative, aesthetic and experiential
aspects. These options are not as daunting as they sound.
The 'aesthetic' approach, for example, looks at religion in
music and art, and the 'experiential' approach at forms of
worship, festival and prayer.

On the whole, the tone of the handbook is rather
negative towards Christianity. This may be an attempt at
compensation for the years when Christianity *was* the
syllabus. It may also be due to nervousness on the part
of the very many Christian advisors on the syllabus and

handbook; they are falling over themselves in their desire not to appear superior or triumphalistic. In spite of the emphasis of the new approach on teaching the religions as they are, and not as they are presented in books, the theological reading matter suggested for teachers is mostly representative of the radical/critical outlook on Christianity. This outlook, as many have pointed out, is largely confined to the universities and bears little resemblance to what the average churchgoer believes or cares about. On the other hand the teacher is advised to consider the extreme fundamentalist point of view, and to present this to the pupils as a balance to the more critical approach. The fundamentalist viewpoint, of course, has a real and growing constituency in the mainstream churches. And yet, one cannot escape the impression that the decision of the compilers to present Christianity in the terms of this dichotomy was a way of absolving them from the problems of the past. Cynically, one can almost imagine the liberal-minded clergy of the conference deciding that the critical approach should be taught *because* it was fashionably critical of Christianity, while being equally fashionably 'open-minded' to other points of view. At the same time Fundamentalism was so clearly insane that it could safely be taught, as a phenomenon, as a religion adopted by and believed in by other people.

The treatment of Christianity throughout is much more critical and defensive than the treatment of other religions. When discussing resource material on Christianity the handbook gives a solemn warning: 'Many of the publications and teaching aids recommended in the following lists are "confessional", that is, produced by Christians for the instruction of people associated with the Christian church, and, therefore, assume belief or commitment on the part of those to whom they are directed . . . "Confessional" material should . . . be presented to pupils only as authentic evidence of Christian belief.'[10] No warning is offered about the resource material for Islam and

Sikhism, in spite of the fact that a number of the books
mentioned are written by Muslims and Sikhs, not merely
as apologetic to the outside world, but as 'confessional'
teaching material for second generation, English-speaking
Asian children.

The critical approach continues in the course outlines
on Christianity. The aim of one of the courses on the life
of Jesus is : 'To help pupils form a critical estimate of the
life and work of Jesus.' But no such critical estimate is
suggested for the life of Mohammed or Guru Nanak. The
aim of a section on Christian beliefs is : '. . . to encourage
pupils to assess what significance belief, or non-belief, in
Jesus may have for them . . . to develop pupils' critical
appreciation of their beliefs so they may see the difficulties
and objections as well as the strengths and weaknesses.'
On the other hand, it is hoped that a study of Islam will :
'Deepen respect for Islam by showing the contribution
made by Islam towards the progress of humanity.' Cool-
ness towards Christianity extends into a study of worship.
Here the aim is : 'To encourage pupils to study critically
the value of prayer and worship for expressing and supporting ways of living.' Apart from the dreary and utilitarian approach to worship suggested by this 'aim', it
contrasts strangely with the aim of one of the courses on
Hinduism, where the aim is unashamedly : 'To communicate the joy and satisfaction that is gained from observing
festivals, and to note the manner in which they give a
natural rhythm to life.'

It is possible of course, to argue that the more critical
approach to Christianity reflects the approach of current
theology. Christian theology has certainly incorporated
'scientific' method into the study of its own origins and
developments to a greater degree than the theology of the
other religions has as yet. And yet there are Christians
other than Biblical fundamentalists who would not share
the critical/radical approach. They will not discount the
importance of Biblical and doctrinal criticism, but they

are unhappy about the blank denial of the supernatural from which much modern theology starts. They are beginning to suspect that what passes for the study of Christianity is, in fact, a study of early Christian psychology and later Christian sociology, in which the Christian claim to revelation is dismissed as pathological. And yet the Birmingham handbook insists that it must be communicated firmly to children that Muslims believe in the divine origin of the Koran. Teachers are not expected to raise or face problems over the belief that the Koran was dictated word for word to Mohammed by the Archangel Gabriel. And yet angels in the New Testament are automatically to be presented as metaphorical or mythological figures. The handbook shows scant concern for Christianity as it is actually believed today (except among conservative evangelicals), and seems much more concerned to use Christianity as a scapegoat for generalized questions about the nature of religion, the function of belief, the objections to religious commitment, etc.

John V. Taylor summarized the difficulties he had with the syllabus and handbook in an article in the magazine *Learning for Living*. He starts by stating his opinion that, whether we like it or not, education is not primarily a process of drawing out the latent capacities of a child. It is *always* an initiation into the moral and cultural values of society: 'It is quite clear that the members of the conference that wrote the Birmingham syllabus and handbook want to see a religious education that will initiate pupils into a pluralist society in a way that will enable them to live in it creatively and with compassion. But, apart from that, into what "stance for living" is their approach likely to initiate a child? To study the handbook in detail with this question in mind is a revealing experience.

'This is essentially an initiation into non-commitment. With great skill the authors have combined a spirit of idealism with a strong emphasis on objectivity. Though there are frequent references to religious experience, this appears to be admitted into the classroom only as some-one else's experience, to be recognized and analytically observed. Such religious education should enable every child to be on the side of the angels without actually believing in them.'[11]

Perhaps this is precisely the aim of the liberal-minded clergy and evangelically-minded humanists. The conference was remarkable for having a humanist representative co-opted on to it. Dr Stopes-Roe has gone on to represent the humanist lobby in debates on RE organized by the Schools' Council. As a result of the failure of the 1974 syllabus, Dr Stopes-Roe has swung the British Humanist Association back into the fight to alter, or repeal, the religious clauses of the 1944 Act. On purely educational grounds, he argues, religious education should be education in stances for living. To go on teaching religion as a phenomenon in its own right is to be biased in favour of the truth of religion. According to Dr Stopes-Roe, the City of Birmingham Education Authority originally accepted this argument. It was only the paranoia of the political conservatives, always looking for 'reds under the beds', and churchmen who wanted to bolster up the privileged position of the churches, that defeated this major step forward in education for living. Now that the forces of reaction have invoked the law to maintain an unfair and unbalanced position, the law must be changed![12]

There is some plausibility in this argument. Dr Stopes-Roe is perfectly accurate when he accuses the church of wanting to maintain privilege at the cost of integrity. The actions of the Birmingham church protest groups were motivated by nostalgia for Christendom rather than Christian principle. But Dr Stopes-Roe's argument, and the handbook which so largely expresses his own point of view, fall down not on political grounds, but on educational ones. First, it is clear that the main objection to the

original syllabus was an objection to the inclusion of
Communism. If there had been no communist options it
is quite likely that the humanist 'stances for living'
philosophy would have been accepted. But if it had been
accepted it would have meant a very radical change
indeed. The humanists seem to want to change the study
of religion into what could be called the study of 'philosophies of life'. But philosophy of life is a very different
subject. It includes disciplines such as logic and the structure of language. It involves study of, for example, the
Greek philosophers, Thomism, the growth of empirical
philosophy and the rise of science. Possibly it should
branch out from its European base and consider Vedanta
and the Chinese philosophy of Taoism. It will try to show
how at different periods and in different cultures man has
understood and perceived reality, what estimates he has
given to his own knowledge, and how his perceptions have
guided him in the formulation of public laws and personal
ethics. Philosophy is certainly akin to religion, and some
religions have developed important philosophies. But the
two are not the same thing. Philosophy has no ritual
dimension, philosophy, quite properly, has no concern
with prayer or worship. There are philosophical writings,
but no sacred books. There are philosophical myths, but
they are free inventions for the purpose of clarification,
not life-giving stories from the past which give meaning
to the present. There is certainly a place for the teaching
of philosophy alongside religion, though some will feel
that it should not be tackled until university level. It will
also occur in small doses in the context of other subjects,
such as science and literature. But simply to suggest that
religion *becomes* philosophy, or worse, *is* philosophy, is
to evade the problem of religion. Religion is concerned
with ultimate issues, with the different answers to the
fundamental questions of existence, which are related to,
but different from, the questions of philosophy: Why

does anything exist at all? Is there any purpose in existence? Is man answerable for what he does with his life?
If so, to whom? etc.[13]

These questions do not go away, and they give rise to
the human phenomenon of religion, which is worthy of
consideration and deep study in its own right. A non-
religious life-stance certainly is not a religion. It might
be a philosophy. But a religion, though it may give rise
to a philosophy, is not, in itself, a philosophy at all. So
the notion of life-stances and 'non-religions' seem more
incoherent than useful, and certainly do nothing to detract
from the argument that religion is worth studying as a
serious academic subject. That does not mean that
Humanism and Communism should be excluded from a
syllabus of RE. The revised syllabus, as we have seen,
allows for them, but in the context of the study of religion.
Both, however, must prove themselves as useful to the
study of religion. Suspicions about the status of Humanism
increase on consideration of the course which originally
appeared in the Birmingham handbook. With the optimistic faith of Eastern Orthodox Christians who hail Plato
as a Christian before Christ because he bore witness to
the immortality of the soul, modern humanists claim
Epicurus as their founding father. Thus Humanism declares
its roots in antiquity. In the Christian era Humanism lay
dormant and Christian faith dominated the intellectual
life of man. The next stage on the humanist journey was
the dawn of empiricism, with its new perspectives on
religion and science. Then came the modern concept of
man derived from a fuller understanding of the geological
time-scale and the process of evolution. Since then,
Humanism has developed a natural morality based on an
interpretation of psychology and anthropology and the
utilitarian theory of ethics. This outline of Humanism is
very English in its bias. It's rather like a course on
Christianity which taught nothing after St Paul but the
history and doctrine of the Church of England. The frame-

work depends on Hobbes, Hume and Darwin, and our own peculiarly English blend of empiricism and pragmatism, undergirded by the doctrine of evolution. No doubt this is an interesting combination, and has born fruit in the lives of a significant number of English men and women. But it is parochial in the extreme, and cannot compete in terms of sheer credibility with Communism and the great religions. The presentation of Humanism would have been greatly strengthened if there had been any attention paid to the significant number of comparative philosophies which start from the assumption that man is the measure of all things. There is no mention of the humanistic teachings of Confucius, nor of early Buddhism, which protested as strongly as Lucretius against superstitious belief in a creator God. There is no mention of Zen, with its radical critique of all religious forms. Nor does the Birmingham handbook pay attention to European movements which have criticized religion in the name of humanity. Maybe it is a fear of being associated with religion, even non-theistic religion, or a fear of the nihilism and depressing realism of the movements associated with Nietsche or Sartre, which prevents their inclusion in the course outline. Marie Curie and Voltaire are mentioned, but they are exceptional. One suspects that the 'Humanism' outlined here is merely the party line of the British Humanist Association. It is not even 'secularism' in the broad sense of the predominating flavour of today's culture. The poverty of 'Humanism' is shown in the fact that a third of one course outline is devoted to the traditional English humanist attack on the concept of a creator God. Here is confirmation of the suspicion that this kind of Humanism is a noisy, but minor and insignificant British Christian heresy. The presentation of Humanism in the Birmingham handbook is not coherent enough to be worthy of study either on religious or educational grounds.

The handbook's section on Communism presents rather

different problems. Lord Soper argued recently that Communism should be on the school timetable because: 'It is unquestionably a religious faith. We shall get into very considerable trouble if we try to distinguish religion and ideology.'[14] On the other hand most communists do not see Communism as a religion at all, but as a non-religion. The handbook shares this attitude, and treats Communism as a non-religion, a secular life-stance, along with Humanism. At this point, of course, the handbook came into conflict with the revised syllabus, which recommended the teaching of 'non-religions' only insofar as they were presented in the context of religion. However, Communism is linked to Humanism in the handbook, sharing its rejection of the supernatural and accepting evolution as the cornerstone of its theory of man. But whereas Humanism places emphasis on the power of individual thought, and sets the happiness and freedom of the individual as the highest goal of man, Communism sees individual thought as arising from material reality. Freedom and happiness are understood as goals for community. Communism therefore is to be presented in the RE class more as a doctrine for changing man and society than as an economic programme or a political manifesto. Here, Communism is being presented as a 'philosophy' in the sense outlined previously. And yet the bulk of the course outline is concerned neither with philosophy nor religion, but with politics and economics. The course concentrates on the Soviet Union, with a small separate section on Communism in Britain.

Perhaps it is significant that there were no communists co-opted to the conference. A more useful approach, and one more appropriate to the revised syllabus, would have been to consider Marxism in some of its more recent flowerings, in China, Latin America and Africa. In all these areas the religious issues are more accessible, and interesting, than in the Soviet Union or Britain. The religious issues in Soviet Russia arise precisely because

Communism has failed to speak to the religious needs of man, and the Christian churches continue to flourish. The dissident movement is closely connected with the need for transcendence. In China, on the other hand, during the period of the cultural revolution, an extraordinary personal cult grew up around the figure of Chairman Mao Tse-Tung. There is evidence that his framed photograph was treated like an icon, and in some cases simple 'prayers' were said to him at the beginning and end of the day. His writings became a sort of scripture, and the application of his 'thought' was commonly held to increase production in field and factory. At this period, Chinese Communism developed a 'mythology' around the person of Mao, glorifying the heroic 'Long March' which signalled Mao's rise to power. The Chinese system put an almost evangelical emphasis on personal conversion and commitment, and testimonies that have been recorded from former members of the bourgeoisie who came to realize their wrong thinking and to identify with the people in their revolutionary struggle have a marked religious flavour. No political prisoner was considered beyond redemption. His guards and fellow-prisoners were expected to criticize him, to bring him to the point of repentance, where he would be able to make a fresh start. The work done by political prisoners has been an important part of the economy. Work was the means by which prisoners could atone for their sins against the people. It was their chance to join in the building up of Socialism.

Some claim that it was Chairman Mao's achievement to change the consciousness of the Chinese people. He has created a new kind of humanity, and the signs of liberalization which have come from the present leadership are signs that the new humanity is now ready to enter into dialogue with the rest of the world. These are serious claims and they have immediate bearing on religion. They raise issues about the need for ritual and myth, true doctrine, atonement and a sacred community.

Here, if anywhere, a case could be made for seeing Communism as a religion. The present swing away from the doctrines and personality of Chairman Mao suggest that the earlier period has come to be regarded as a time of excess. There is a conscious effort on the part of the Chinese Communist Party to de-mythologize the past. To protest against religion in the name of a purer, simpler doctrine has always been a feature of religious history.

Another area where the relationship between Marxism and religion could be explored is the Third World. In the predominantly Roman Catholic countries of Latin America a new kind of Christian theology is being created. It is revolutionary in content, committed to the overthrow of the frequently oppressive and unstable regimes which hold power. The Christian hope of these people is firmly rooted in the Bible. It is the story of the exodus which gives ground for hope – the story of how God rescued his people, by revolution, from oppression and slavery in Egypt. Marxist Christians also see grounds for hope in the New Testament proclamation of the Kingdom of God. The combination of Marxism with Christian theology is a reminder of the influence of the Bible on Karl Marx, and on other theoretical Marxists like Ernst Bloch. This leads to the question of whether Communism, like Humanism, can be seen as a Jewish-Christian heresy, though a very much more significant one. A course on Communism which approached it from some of these perspectives would be far more credible in the context of RE than the one offered by the Birmingham handbook. It would not be outside the terms of the law, nor would it be merely presenting Communism as a 'philosophy of life'.

While the syllabus was being modified the Conservative council succeeded in having the courses on Humanism and Communism deleted from the handbook. It was perhaps unfortunate that they neglected to read the handbook first, since their ruling only removed course outlines for the senior age group. The Conservative council thus ensured that the secularist viewpoint could be presented in schools in Birmingham to the under twelves only.

What was the overall influence of the Birmingham syllabus and handbook? In spite of the inconsistencies between the two, the new approach met with a good deal of support. More recent papers on RE from the Schools Council have outlined a broadly similar approach. The Religious Education Council has declared itself in favour of the new RE. The Christian churches, too, have been vocal in their support. There were, of course, no fewer than twenty representatives of the Christian churches appointed to the original Birmingham conference. But, since then, working groups from Anglican and Free churches have fallen in with the general commendations of the new RE. A discussion document produced by the Free Church Federal Council's Education Committee states: 'Religious Education, under our terms, becomes a proper study of the various ways in which men have sought to answer the fundamental questions about life; the historical setting of the world religions and their influence upon history and cultural practises which have developed out of them; a basic knowledge of the facts and their interpretations associated with the religions; and a critical appraisal of all these factors without which no educational process is complete.'[15]

But not all Christian bodies have accepted the changes so uncritically. The Birmingham syllabus itself was challenged by the then Bishop of Birmingham and by an Anglican organization. The Order of Christian Unity has offered a continual critique of the new RE. Its campaign against the erosion of Christianity in schools is linked to campaigns against abortion and euthanasia and the irresponsibility of the media. The opponents of the new RE present a cluster of arguments. These start in the continued assertion that Christianity is the bedrock of our culture. If education is an initiation into a culture and a set of cultural values, then it must be rooted in Christian-

ity. The RE class is the obvious space on the timetable
in which Christianity should be taught. That was the whole
intention of the 1944 Act. The problem of teaching RE
to immigrant children has been greatly misunderstood.
Most immigrant families accept the fact that they are
going to have to integrate, to some extent, with British
culture, and would not object to learning about religion
in that context. The withdrawal clause protects their
children from compulsory attendance if the classes are
really found unsuitable. The size of the problem has also
been misrepresented. The number of non-Christian immigrants in schools is probably less than a quarter of a
million. In addition there are some thirteen thousand
Jewish children, some of whom are educated in Jewish
schools. This means that there are only just over a quarter
of a million non-Christian immigrant children out of nine
million within the state system.

These arguments are not entirely fair. They fail to
reckon with the concentration of immigrant children
within particular areas. They also fail to reckon with the
way in which other religions are slowly becoming part
of the everyday world. 'Christian' Britain does not exist
in isolation. Children see the other side of the globe on
television screens. Communication between different
cultures is almost certain to increase rather than decrease.
This is, I suspect, precisely the fear of some of those who
criticize the new RE. They feel it represents an anarchic
spirit, a throwing away of distinctive values in a confusing
world. Hence the insistence of the Order of Christian
Unity that RE teachers should be committed Christians.
Only Christians can hand on the tradition with sympathy
and conviction. Associated with this is the fear many
teachers and parents have of particular losses. Parents
who rarely pray are anxious because their children do
not learn the Lord's Prayer at school. They can no longer
recite the Ten Commandments. Surely something is
missing?

Others fear the loss of Biblical knowledge, and particularly, the passing away of the Authorized Version of the Bible and the Prayer Book. Surely these are classics of our heritage, and their loss is a tragedy? This argument is rather similar to the argument for the general teaching of classics in schools. There is much in European culture which is more easily understood through the framework of a classical education, the structure of our grammar and language being a significant example. Similarly, there is much in history and literature which is more or less incomprehensible without a fairly thorough knowledge of the Bible and of Christian history. Without some knowledge of the classics and the Old Testament how will children make any sense of Milton, Chaucer and Shakespeare? How will they understand medieval Europe and the issues of the Reformation?

There is some strength in these arguments, though they are defensive arguments, and they have nothing to do with the teaching of religion in its own right or for its own sake. But they are sometimes used to cover the more general protest against the secularization of RE that the Birmingham syllabus is thought to represent.

But there is one point on which supporters of the new RE and their opponents agree, and that is that RE is in a mess. It is still, in most schools, a low-priority subject. There is still a chronic shortage of qualified teachers. This is not helped by the fact that it is difficult for most RE teachers to get very far in the struggle for promotion. RE posts are not available at the highest teaching grades except in a very few cases. Faced with this dilemma the new RE calls for a massive expansion in RE training. It requires higher qualifications and a broader range of knowledge than RE has ever demanded in the past. Faced with the demands of the Birmingham handbook, it is clear that the new RE cannot be confined to one lesson a week. There is probably a need for a special RE room, just as many schools have geography rooms, where maps, posters and other visual aids can be housed, and a library built up.

At the same time, the Order of Christian Unity calls on the churches to present the teaching of RE as a serious Christian vocation to their members. They also request a government inquiry into the current provision for RE teaching in county schools, and they deplore the decline of religious education departments training RE teachers for the future. They suggest that there should be a much closer inspection of religious teaching in individual schools, and that those failing to provide adequate RE should be reported to the relevant authorities for breaking the law.

Cynically, one may wonder whether both sides of this debate are being rather unrealistic in their hope for a massive new investment in RE. In a secularized society it is not surprising that the teaching of RE continues to be a low priority. It has just managed to make itself credible in educational terms; can those involved in RE really hope for anything more? In the arguments for or against the new RE there still seems to be the suggestion that RE is special and different, too important to be treated as any other subject. Even in the Birmingham handbook there is plenty of evidence that the old, triumphalistic approach has not died. This is not to be found in the treatment of religious topics. There, as we have seen, the course adopts the scientific paradigm of observation and empirical analysis. Religion is a phenomenon to be studied, and in the case of Christianity, to be studied with the cold eye of detachment. But the courses on religions only take up half the space in the handbook. The rest, as we have seen, is devoted to general topics of relevance to the individual and society. This has gained far less attention and critical comment than the approach to religions. It is really the inheritance of problem-centred RE. The implication is that RE still has a special and central place in the life of the school. It is the class where moral issues are raised and discussed, the class which is most concerned with the child's development as a 'whole' person. The course outlines offered by Birmingham on individual and community life seem designed to increase social awareness and sensitivity. They are a preparation for responsible citizenship. They encourage children to think about personal morality. They introduce children to some of the major social and moral controversies of today. Yet it seems strange that such topics should be considered in isolation. For the course outlines are concerned with life today, and that should be the concern of the whole school. It is either a reflection of latent chauvinism on the part of religious educationists or of dire cynicism on the part of the schools that 'moral' education should still be hived off into RE.

On the whole, I accept the argument that education is more an initiation into society rather than the development of untrammelled individuality. All that is included in 'moral' education should be the responsibility of the whole school. This is what a 'school ethos' or 'school spirit' is all about. There is a long tradition of regarding moral education as a sub-division of RE, but that started from the time when RE itself was the expression of religious commitment on the part of the school community. Now that RE has been secularized, moral education belongs no more to it than any other subject. RE has lost its special quality, but it may be on the way to gaining its credibility. But it cannot stand or fall with other subjects until it has given up its claims to be different. That is not to say that there are no areas of moral concern which are relevant to RE. There are. They are those problems and issues which arise naturally from teaching children about religion; death, for example, or the morality of evangelism. But to assume such an extensive responsibility for the moral and social development of children seems misguided.

The new RE, however, seems firmly set on its course. Those who support it accept its two purposes without apparently noticing that they are mutually incompatible. As far as the religions go, they are to be studied 'phenomenologically', as an aspect of human experience, usually the experience of other people. As far as moral education goes, the RE class is still unique and special, shouldering a heavy burden, which is apparently beyond the time or resources of more academic subjects. To bring the children on to the side of the angels without actually believing in them – that appears to be the purpose of the new RE. The aim is not very far from that of the British Humanist Association, in spite of its sulks over the Birmingham syllabus, and it has been accepted without a murmur by spokesmen from most of the Christian churches.

Autumn 1977

Marani Mehta was finding school difficult. Though her English was good, there was so much that was strange to her, so much that was different from what she had expected. At the mission school in Delhi she had learnt that English children were Christians, they believed in God and Jesus. But other children in her class here said Jesus Christ as a swear word. She had been taught to pray to God when she woke up in the morning. But the English children did not seem to care about God much. Or their families. Once a week they had a class on religion. The teacher thought she would stay out because she was a Hindu, he said, but her mother and father said she must stay in. Then she was confused because they talked about Jesus just as the teachers had done at her school in Delhi. But in Delhi they believed in Jesus, and here they did not. What a strange country this was!

The Reverend Barry Spindle was delighted that he had

been asked to be a member of the Conference to revise the RE syllabus. He had been angling and politicing for this for two years. He fingered the letter of invitation with glee. Then he rang his great friend Dick Marcus, who told him he had been invited to the conference meetings as a humanist observer.

'That's marvellous, Dick. I thought I was going to have to argue your case for you.' 'Oh, you can do it much better than me!'

'I've always said Christians make the best humanists; and of course humanists are a hell of a lot better Christians than most Christians.'

'You won't get me into the fold *that* way.'

'Dick, I'd *hate* you in the fold. What about the revolution anyway?'

'Well, have you any ideas?'

'Look, why don't you come round some time and we'll do a bit of plotting . . .'

Roger Short cursed his ill-luck. He was good at appointing staff. Usually. He was bad at dismissing them. It had taken eleven years to get rid of that dreadful missionary woman. And now. It was always religion that was the problem. He thought the bright young Cambridge graduate was just what he wanted. Strong socialist, working-class background. Good degree in history, and theology. The headmaster groaned. Never have anyone *too* bright on the staff, he mused. For the bright young man had ideas about RE. He wanted more time on the timetable. He wanted an assistant. He wanted more money. Money! What do you need money for in RE? He talked of new books, films and tapes, travel, outside speakers. It was preposterous. It was as if RE was a serious subject. Come back, Irene Potter. Please!

NOTES

1. *Teenage Religion*: appendix A
2. Comments recorded for *Young People's Beliefs*
3. *Discovering an Approach*: Macmillan Education 1977
4. Ibid.
5. Ibid.
6. Ibid.
7. *Agreed Syllabus of Religious Instruction*: putatively adopted by the Education Committee of the City of Birmingham District Council, 7 May 1974
8. *Agreed Syllabus of Religious Instruction*, City of Birmingham District Council Education Committee, 1975
9. *Living Together*, a teacher's handbook of suggestions for religious education, City of Birmingham Education Committee, 1976, p. a 6
10. Ibid. p. c 54
11. 'Initiation into Agnosticism': John V. Taylor, in *Learning for Living*. Summer 1976, p. 130
12. See: *Objective Fair and Balanced*: British Humanist Association, Autumn 1975
13. See (4)
14. Lord Soper was speaking at the 1976 Methodist Conference at Preston
15. *Religious Education in County Schools*: The Free Church Federal Council, June 1976

CHAPTER FOUR

A Right to Pray?

An independent girls' school, previously direct grant, files into hall for assembly on the first day of a new term. The headmistress, wearing academic dress, mounts the platform and addresses the school, welcoming them back after the holidays. She then moves to the lectern and reads a lesson from the New Testament. The whole school then joins, heads bowed, in the Lord's Prayer. The headmistress reads her two favourite collects from the Book of Common Prayer. Then the uniformed ranks of girls, eight hundred strong, join in singing the school hymn: 'Let us now praise famous men'.

The top three forms of a large comprehensive squeeze into the gym for prayers. No one prays, but there is a reading from Spike Milligan followed by Simon and Garfunkel's 'Bridge over Troubled Water' played on a record player. A senior master gives out a notice about new dinner arrangements.

Assembly begins at a primary school when the RE teacher rings an Eastern-looking brass gong. Standing in front of the school he announces that it is the Muslim feast of Id El Fitr. He reads an appropriate passage from the Koran and shows the children a mounted display of Id El Fitr cards which some of the Pakistani children have brought from home. He cues the music teacher who begins to play the first line of 'God is Love'.

In the geography room of a boys' public school a member of the fifth form is presenting facts and figures about the latest cyclone to hit the West coast of India. He has a selection of leaflets from Christian Aid and Oxfam and has pinned a stark black and white poster of starving children on the notice board behind him. When he has finished the boys sit in silence for about a minute.

In a Roman Catholic Junior school the parish priest has arrived to say the weekly lunch-time Mass. As the four members of staff make their communion, the children look on, crossing themselves as instructed, joining in with the hymn and the amens at the ends of the prayers, hands together, eyes closed.

The 1944 Education Act requires that the school day shall begin with 'an act of corporate worship'. Most schools had, in practice, assembled for prayers and hymns since the last century: 'Religious observances, as they were called, usually took place every day. The syllabus of religious instruction used in schools was really a catechism, and since the catechism would contain items such as the Ten Commandments, the Lord's Prayer and the Apostles' Creed it supplied the needs of both instruction and worship . . . the schools did not worship to facilitate instruction; they instructed in order to facilitate the worship.'[1]

Worship was a natural function of the school that regarded itself as a Christian community. Worship was the expression of its corporate identity. What could be more appropriate than the offering of thanks and praise and prayer to God on the part of a community that was part of God's people? There was considerable controversy, however, over the place of worship in the 1944 Education Act. Though the act was only making statutory what was generally accepted in practice, many felt there was something undesirable about requiring an act of worship to take place by law. Some Christians however, were delighted at the inclusion of the clause: 'Now and for the years to come, nothing less than the repeal of section 25 of the Education Act 1944 . . . can prevent the daily offering to Almighty God of the worship of the school-children of England and Wales. Meanwhile, "the voice of prayer is never silent, nor dies the strain of praise away".'[2]

Archbishop Temple was not entirely happy about the worship clause, though he eventually decided in favour of it. The withdrawal clause safeguarded the consciences of those who honestly could not participate in Christian worship: 'On the whole . . . I am inclined to think it is best to leave the clause in the bill and trust that it will be administered with tact and gentleness. Of course, it is quite true that for prayer to be taken in a perfunctory or hypocritical way can only do harm. On the other hand, the majority of people try to do well what they do at all, and there will be a considerable number who are led to include prayers because of the statutory requirement who would otherwise let them slide. I think teachers are a little liable to ignore the fact that while it is objectionable to force the teachers to conduct prayers against their consciences, it is also objectionable to force children to omit prayers for the sake of the teachers' consciences.'[3]

Compulsory school worship, however, has never ceased to be controversial. The humanist and secularist organizations have waged a continual war against it, and, over the years, more and more Christians have come to share their objections. The chief objection is that it puts some teachers and head teachers in a hypocritical position. It is argued that the conscience clause excuses non-Christian teachers from participating in assembly. But many teachers feel that opting out of assembly makes them look as if they are unwilling to be part of the school at the time when it is most conscious of its corporate identity. Some have feared that unwillingness to lead or participate in assembly may affect their chances of promotion. It is a particular problem for head teachers, who usually shoulder the main burden of responsibility for organizing

school worship. If they are agnostic or atheist, what are
they to do? Temple seems to suggest that they swallow
their objections, and 'take' traditional prayers on behalf
of the children. But this may come from Temple's own
inability, as a man who had never experienced doubt,
to take unbelief seriously. He sometimes seemed to regard
unbelief more as a moral failing, or a lapse of concentration, than a serious 'stance for living'. With the current
changes in RE teaching the humanist attack on school
worship has intensified. Humanists find it intolerable that
RE teachers who have tried to teach in an 'open' way
should have their efforts undermined by having to participate in collective worship. At the same time it is clear
from the report on a recent survey conducted on behalf
of the Assistant Masters' Association that a considerable
proportion of RE teachers will have nothing to do with
organizing assembly.[4]

As the idea that all schools were Christian communities
began to break down those who supported school worship
began to look for other grounds on which to justify it.
Some saw the assembly with its act of worship as a useful
opportunity for evangelism, more effective than the RE
class: 'It is because in worship these attributes of God
are simply taken for granted and not argued or deliberately
taught, that worship is the most powerful medium of all
for communicating dogmatic truth.' J. G. Williams has
been heavily criticized for that remark by fellow-
Christians and by humanists, who felt he was commending
worship as an underhand form of indoctrination. But his
argument for maintaining school worship on these grounds
falls down because the internal logic is wrong. It is not
the purpose of worship to communicate dogmatic truth.
It may succeed in doing that, but that is not its primary
purpose.

A more coherent collection of arguments for the main-
tenance of school worship is presented in *The Fourth 'R'*
— the Durham Report on Religious Education (1970).[5]

The report concentrates on the educational value of worship. Worship is a major element in all religions. If religious education is to continue in schools then it is essential that pupils should have some initiation into the experience of worship. It is too much to expect that the majority of children will have much opportunity for worship outside school, so worship must be laid on inside school hours.

The problem with this argument is that, once again, it is justifying worship by what is, in fact, one of its by-products. It is not the purpose of worship to initiate children into an educationally useful experience. The argument seems to suggest that worship should be put on or 'staged' for the children's benefit. It is a kind of religious Punch and Judy show with a hidden moral in the last line.

The Durham report continues with a new argument. All human beings seem to have a need to participate in religious, or quasi-religious ritual. The daily act of worship is an opportunity to do this. It is also clear that most people need periods of quiet and reflection and occasions for communal celebration.

This argument is not really about worship at all. Ritual can be secular. Reflection and celebration do not automatically refer to the divine. Worship *may* help to meet such needs as we have for reflection and celebration, but that is not what worship is for in the first instance. It also seems to be the case that there are many people in our society who feel a deep unease about corporate ritual. They find it depersonalizing and intrusive, and certainly do not feel they 'need' it. It is possible that school assemblies may have reinforced this unease, and set up permanent inhibitions in some people about corporate worship in any form. If one of the aims of worship in schools was to encourage pupils to participate in the Christian worship of the churches, then it may well have had precisely the opposite effect.

The Durham report suggests next that a religious assembly gives an opportunity for committed Christians among the staff and pupils to dedicate themselves to God and pray for the day ahead. Non-Christians are provided at the same time with a chance to re-affirm their personal ideals and values.

Certainly an act of Christian worship may be helpful to Christians, though there is no reason why Christians should dedicate themselves to God for the day at a time when the whole school is present. There is nothing to stop the Christian members of a school community meeting in some other context to offer prayer and praise. At the same time non-Christians are unlikely to find an act of Christian worship conducive to re-affirming their personal (non-Christian) values. It is rather like expecting a clergyman to say matins silently at a public meeting of the National Secular Society.

The last argument presented in the Durham report suggests that there are still occasions in public life where worship takes place, and it is an advantage for children to have had some experience of worship before having to attend a wedding, a funeral, or a Remembrance Day service. This may be true, but again, it is hardly the point. There is nothing to stop children learning about weddings and funerals in class. They should be taken occasionally to observe religious services in local churches; this is part of their religious education. But it does not follow that this justifies a daily act of Christian worship for the whole school.

The Durham report goes on to consider the arguments for keeping the daily act of worship compulsory. Here, the reasons are slightly different. It is suggested that if the legal requirement were removed worship would wither away through hostility, timidity or sloth on the part of the teachers. Against this the compilers of the report are aware of the fact that a compulsory assembly can easily degenerate into: 'a mindless routine leading to formless indifferentism'.

But even with the statute in force, school worship *has* withered away completely in many schools. The Assistant Masters' Association survey reveals that nine-tenths of the eleven hundred schools which took part are not holding assemblies that meet the requirement of the act: 'It is evident that the traditional act of worship is not being held in many schools.'[6]

A father in Sheffield was recently so incensed by the fact that fifteen Sheffield schools were failing to provide religious assembly that he considered taking legal action against them. It is, of course, notoriously difficult to prove that a school is breaking the law in this respect. It would virtually require a written statement from the head teacher to the effect that he had no intention of conducting assemblies that conformed with the Act. As it is, many schools are actually unable to hold corporate worship because there is no room or hall large enough to hold everybody. This has happened frequently when two or more schools have come together to form a single comprehensive, using the already existing school buildings. The act allows for this possibility: 'The arrangements made therefore shall provide for a single act of worship attended by all such pupils unless, in the opinion of the local authority, or in the case of a voluntary school, of the managers or governors thereof, the school premises are such as to make it impracticable to assemble them for that purpose.'[7] In practice this provision has provided an escape clause for those who are unwilling, or find it inconvenient, to hold religious assemblies.

The Durham report goes on to suggest that a daily act of worship, 'expresses the corporate life of the school, serves as a useful agency for transmitting school values, and provides a mood-setting formality for the start of the day'. At the same time, the compilers are all too aware that the present requirements can engender 'boredom, apathy, unease and even resentment and hostility.'. The AMA survey confirms this. If it is clear that the assembly is merely being used as a place to express school values the 'worship' becomes irrelevant. The survey reports 'a general feeling that the so-called act of corporate worship is a platform for the school ethos rather than any religious ethos, and valuable as such'. The survey goes on to quote comments to the effect that assembly is useful because of its effects on the pupils' behaviour : 'Behaviour is noticeably worse on Monday when there is no assembly.' So is religious assembly, then, no more than 'an institutional form of child-control through coalition with God'? Useful as such an exercise might be it has little to do with worship.

The Durham report claims that there are two aspects to worship, the expressive and the didactic. The justification it offers for maintaining compulsory worship in schools depend almost entirely on the didactic aspect. Assembly has a teaching function and can be justified on educational grounds. But the Durham report was produced when the secularization of RE was only at the beginning. Its assumptions are criticized by John Hull in *School Worship – an Obituary*. He claims that worship should be seen primarily as a response. This response involves an inner and outer side. Outwardly there is ritual, singing, formal reading, praying. Inwardly there is commitment to an appropriate life-style and an ethical standpoint. Worship is a transitive verb. It is impossible to worship in the abstract. There must be an object of worship. Worship therefore involves beliefs. In an atmosphere of cool, academic detachment, in the study, library or classroom, it is possible to reflect on conflicting images of deity. But in worship the believer seeks to respond to the God he actually believes in, the God who has evoked worship in him. In worship he affirms his belief, celebrates and adores his God, communicates his inner needs to his God, and in consequence, re-directs himself and his life to serving his God better. The value of worship is not to be judged by results. There is no clearly discernable value to worship at all. It is the offering to God of what is worthy of him in terms of praise, thanksgiving and commitment.

Hull goes on to argue that there is an inevitable tension between worship and education. The purpose of education is to enable children to enquire for themselves, to analyse, criticize, and evaluate. Education involves grasping the principles behind a body of knowledge, it is not just the handing down of a body of knowledge from one generation to the next. By grasping the principles of a body of knowledge the pupil is enabled to acquire new knowledge for himself. Worship and education are in tension because: 'Worship is committed to its content and is passionate and adoring, while education is detached from its content and is enquiring and reflective.'[8] There is, therefore, an intolerable tension between the new RE, which is 'educational' and school worship, which assumes the truths that education is supposed to question. To justify worship on educational grounds is to compromise the detachment of education and to devalue worship. It is to assume that a child can, at the same time, participate and not participate, which, of course, is impossible.

Hull's argument is a Christian version of the argument of the humanists. On the whole it is convincing, though he seems to overstate the view that worship has no didactic element. It is one thing to refuse to justify worship on educational grounds, it is quite another not to acknowledge that worship can educate. Many clergy have long suspected that congregations acquire more theology from hymns than from instructive sermons. It is also important to notice how uncritically Hull accepts the view of education as a value-free process in which the child is taught to analyse and criticize. This model is one taken from the natural sciences. But it is less appropriate for the teaching of music or literature. It is clear that Hull sees RE as having more in common with the sciences than the arts; he is at one with those who take the 'phenomenological' approach, inspired by sociology, which usually regards itself as a science.

However, the conclusion of his argument is inevitable. With the humanists, he asserts that compulsory school worship must be ended.

On the whole, though, educationists are not ready to fight the political battles of killing off worship in schools. The apathy and unease of many schools is having its own effect, while the escape clause about the suitability of premises prevents head teachers from going outside the law. Meanwhile, the attempt goes on to justify some form of worship on educational grounds and to harangue the schools for lapsing into routine, putting up with boring presentation, and generally displaying a lack of imagination.

A Schools Council working paper, after a careful survey of assemblies in primary schools, concludes that there is a great deal of uncertainty about the function and purpose of assembly. Some run on traditional patterns, with a Bible reading, a hymn and a prayer. Others seem to be purely social occasions, when notices are given out, and the head teacher offers a few moral admonitions. The report concludes: 'We suggest with some trepidation . . . that the time has come to resolve this ambivalence by giving up the notion that a county primary school assembly ought to be an act of Christian worship in the commonly accepted sense of the word.'[9] There are a number of reasons offered for this conclusion. The main one is that primary school children are unable to grasp the theological presuppositions of worship. Traditional liturgical forms can have little meaning for them. However, the paper suggests that it might be significant for the children if believing teachers occasionally said prayers, though there must be no insistence that the children join in. There is also educational value in singing carefully chosen hymns together. The children will not understand the words, but there is a benefit in making melody and rhythm and sharing in something that some of the adults find important.

A companion paper on secondary schools makes no recommendations for the future of assembly. It does describe, however, some of the educationally useful features of assembly, and concludes that, in some form, it still has a strong hold.

The strangest and most contorted arguments in favour of religious assembly are in the Birmingham handbook *Living Together*. Assembly is affirmed as a sign of the unity and mutual responsibility of the school community. Assembly understood in this way is not the same thing as the traditional act of corporate worship, but it may be used as a context in which the statutory act of worship may take place. Worship is defined, with echoes of John Hull, as: 'A response to that which is of ultimate concern, involving a sense of relationship with its transcendent object.'[10] Collective worship is a communal activity, but the inward response is private, and may or may not take place in the context of the corporate act. The educationally valuable aspects of corporate worship are then listed. The handbook then goes on to state that the purpose of worship in a religious community is to nurture faith. Until recently the county school has been seen as a religious community, and the purpose of worship was clear. At the same time the purpose of RE was to instruct children in the faith. But now, county schools are not seen as religious communities. Pupils do not all believe the same things, and they should not be treated as if they did. Teachers and pupils are searching for a common ground on which to express shared ideals and aspirations: 'This open-minded approach to worship is in keeping with the spirit of our handbook, which assumes that though it is appropriate to affirm shared values and beliefs in county schools, these should nevertheless be exposed for explana-

tion and criticism. Pupils should not be required to participate in acts of worship which cause them to affirm, even
by implication, that which they do not believe.'[11]

The handbook presents a heroic attempt to meet the
requirements of the law without compromising its own
commitment to open-ended agnosticism, but it is doubtful
how far the suggestion offered can really be counted as
'worship'. Prayer is to be allowed in assemblies, but
prayers are to be read rather than prayed. Hymn singing
is allowed, but hymns which include personal professions
of belief are to be avoided. Readings are to be allowed
from any inspirational source, but those who read must
do so voluntarily. There may be affirmations of belief,
but there must also be affirmation of non-religious beliefs.
There may be affirmations of moral values, but assembly
should be one of the major opportunities for exposing
them to explanation and criticism.

It could be argued that the handbook's approach is well
within the spirit of the 1944 Act. The act requires corporate worship. It does not, and cannot, legislate for the
correct religious response from the individual. But even
the educationists who worked on the handbook do not
invoke this argument. John Hull would see the Birmingham suggestion as a way of bringing children to 'the
threshold of worship'. He does not regard this as worship
proper, which requires an individual response. And yet,
the Birmingham handbook cannot be seen to be suggesting
that schools break the law. It is important that what
they offer should be compatible with the statutory requirement. It has to appear to be worship in the eyes of the
law, even though the handbook itself is committed, on
educational grounds, to the view that the county school
cannot, and should not be, a worshipping community:
'The kind of celebration envisaged thus takes the com-
ponents of traditional worship and applies them to the
secular setting of the county school . . . it will draw upon
moral and religious expressions from many sources and

traditions and use many forms of expression to provide a rich and stimulating experience for the pupils and a context in which true personal worship can take place.'[12]

There is a fundamental dishonesty about this approach. It approves the continuation of 'worship-elements' in assembly, on educational grounds. At the same time it presents these in the hope that, in the eyes of the law, this will fulfil the requirement for corporate worship. What are the pupils supposed to think? The likelihood is that, not knowing anything else, they will regard this syncretistic mish-mash as worship proper. They would be justified in doing so from the point of view of the law. And yet the whole burden of the Birmingham approach is to separate the private and the public, to turn the act of corporate worship into a public arena of debate and discussion, in the vain hope that individuals might be moved to use that occasion for making a personal response of worship.

The compilers of the Birmingham handbook can hardly be unaware of the ambiguity of their position. They would probably welcome a change in the law.

The argument that religious assembly would fall into disuse if it was not backed by law, has been shown to be false. Religious assembly *is* falling into disuse, and, where it is maintained, there is pressure to radically alter its character, while retaining the word 'worship' in order to stay within the letter of the law. The only way that real worship can be maintained in schools is for it to become voluntary. This is not quite the contradiction that it appears. But it does mean that the school ethos becomes formally separated from acts of worship which may or may not occur. Worship would cease to be the communal activity of the whole school in which it expresses its ideological identity. It could be argued that the withdrawal clause already makes attendance at school prayers voluntary. But in practice this is not the case, as the humanists have pointed out. Withdrawal from worship involves the written request of the parent. It puts the child in the awkward position of having to 'drop out' of an activity intended for the whole school. It is also regarded as a fixed decision. Once a child is 'registered' as a Jehovah's Witness or an atheist, he is not expected to have anything to do with the worship of the school. He cannot adopt a floating status, which may be just what he himself wants to do. In the county school attendance at worship should depend on the free and voluntary decision of pupils themselves. In the primary school the choice should be put to parents. This seems to be the only tolerable solution in schools where pupils come from a number of different traditions. The Christian members of the school community should organize their own worship, they could meet for prayers either before or after school hours. They should be open to the possibility that others may wish to attend. They should be free to arrange visits from local clergy, and they might have the occasional communion service. Such an event might be used by the RE department as an example of genuine Christian worship. Already in some schools in the Midlands the school hall is given over to the Muslim community on Friday afternoons; the local iman comes and conducts prayers for the Muslim children. If other children are curious, there is no reason why they should not attend. This is making educational use of school worship without implying that its primary function is educational. The integrity of the worship, and the worshippers, is not compromised. It is also possible that the school will want to organize its own voluntary worship for particularly important festivals. Prayer and hymn singing would be quite appropriate at these. Schools may want carol services or services for a founder's day. All these are permissible, but in the county school they should be voluntary. This means, of course, that in the county school worship is to be separated from assembly. The point of assembly is that the whole school is gathered together. Assemblies can be compulsory in the same way that lessons are. Assemblies are probably necessary in most schools from time to time. It is important that there is a wide forum for considering matters of common interest and raising issues of importance for the community as a whole. Here, the school can seek, and express, its ideological unity and diversity insofar as it has them. But this gathering does not require an act of worship to make it valid. It is in fact rather dishonest to create a form of mock-worship in which all can participate without being obliged to display commitment.

It is sometimes argued that any change in the law as it stands would bring intolerable local pressure to bear on head teachers, who would be subject to propaganda both from religious and humanist groups. But the present law is hardly effective in keeping a balance between the different pressure groups. Even at the time of the act the worship clause was controversial. Making worship voluntary would do something to balance the pressure from those who want worship abolished altogether and those who want it strengthened. It is unfortunate that those who argue politically for the retention of the statute do not appreciate that the status of and interest in school worship would almost certainly rise as soon as it ceased to be compulsory.

Norman St John Stevas, in supporting compulsory worship, has stated recently: 'I believe that the overwhelming majority of parents in Britain want to see religious education continue in our schools and for their children to have the opportunity of praying together.' The real issue is whether this 'opportunity' should be guaranteed by law, or whether it should be the unwritten responsibility of pupils, parents and staff who share a religious commitment.

The situation is rather different in church schools and independent schools. Independent schools are not bound at all by the religious provisions of the 1944 act. Church schools are in an ambiguous position which will be explored in the next chapter. But some church schools and independent schools can make a real claim to be religious communities in the way that modern county schools cannot. They may have strong connections with the church, and may see their role as that of offering a Christian education. This is clearly understood by the parents, and either desired by them or tolerated for the sake of other educational advantages. In these cases it is more appropriate for the whole school to gather in an act of Christian worship. It is not necessary that all those who attend such services should be committed Christians, only that they are willing to participate in an expression of the school's corporate identity as a Christian community. There is nothing hypocritical in a church school or an independent school choosing to regard itself as a Christian community, and requiring teachers and pupils to attend at acts of worship where the school identifies itself as such. What is hypocritical is the belief that bringing children to the 'threshold of worship' should 'count' as worship in the eyes of the law, though not, of course, in the eyes of teachers and educationists.

So, severing the link between worship and assembly should safeguard the school from hypocrisy and maintain the possibility of genuine worship on school premises. It also safeguards against the danger of syncretism, a very real danger, which is not considered by the compilers of the Birmingham handbook. It means that the distinction between education and worship, so passionately advocated by John Hull, is maintained, without reducing the occasions on which worship is 'available' for observation.

There is nothing particularly novel about this solution. Something rather like it has been practised in some schools for years. Sometimes, alongside 'prayers' for the majority, schools have held Catholic and Jewish prayers as well. Now such arrangements were clearly compromising the principle of corporate worship by which every pupil was required to attend 'prayers' unless he had been withdrawn by parents. Holding separate acts of worship makes the withdrawal clause unnecessary. Making all school prayers voluntary is merely extending the principle. There would be no 'general prayers' for all but Catholics, Jews and Jehovah's Witnesses to attend. Nor would school notices be attached to these small gatherings. The place for notices is assembly, when the whole school, or sections of it, come together.

There is one intriguing suggestion which arises out of the debate. One argument in favour of religious assembly is that it provides a time for quiet and reflection which otherwise get left out of the normal school day. Perhaps instead of a slot on the timetable for quietness, schools could provide a quiet room, to be used for private thought and meditation. It should not be in any sense a chapel, and should not contain any explicit religious symbols. It could contain books, but the setting should be informal. The only rules, which would need to be ruthlessly enforced, would be silence and a degree of stillness.

As educationists seem determined to define education in narrower and narrower terms it is necessary to state that the quiet room would have no educational function whatever.

NOTES

1. *School Worship – an Obituary* : p. 11
2. *The Teacher's Handbook to a Book of Morning Worship* : C. L. Berry, J. M. Dent 1946, p. 11. Quoted in *School Worship – an Obituary* : p. 24
3. *William Temple – Archbishop of Canterbury* : pp. 574-5
4. *Religious Education* : report by Assistant Masters' Association, 1978
5. *The Fourth 'R'*
6. *Education Act 1944* : part II, 25, 7 & 8, HMSO

7.   *School Worship – an Obituary* : p. 102
8.   *School Worship – an Obituary* : p. 62
9.   *Religious Education in Primary Schools* : Schools Council
     Working Paper 44, Evans/Methuen Educational 1972, p. 66
10. *Living Together* : p. 2
11. Ibid. p. 3
12. Ibid. p. 4

CHAPTER FIVE

God, Faith and Privilege

The church in the past has been committed to education as part of its mission to society: 'It is a Christian's concern for the wholeness of the human being, for the quality of the common life, for the direction in which man goes, that turns him towards education now, and sets him inside it — and will not let him disengage.'[1]

There are two aspects to the Christian involvement with education. On the one hand Christians are concerned with the development of the whole personality. From a Christian point of view education fails if it is only concerned with academic achievement, or the acquiring of specific technical skills, or the ability to make good relationships. True human wholeness involves all these, and much more. But Christianity goes further even than this in stating that true human wholeness is crowned by a relationship with Christ. The final aim of Christian education is wholeness and maturity in Christ. That is not to say that non-Christian individuals cannot achieve wholeness or integration, nor is it to suggest that Christians, by virtue of being Christians, have already achieved full wholeness and harmony. It is only to say that from the Christian point of view Christ is the fulfilment of all that is highest and best in man, and Christian learning, or discipleship, is a life-long process in which the individual grows into the image and likeness of God in Christ.

But Christian education also involves learning the faith. For children, this means absorbing a Christian atmosphere at church and home, taking part in worship, becoming a member of the church through the rites of baptism or confirmation, or the equivalent, and beginning to learn about the Bible. For adults, Christian education means a growing awareness of the relevance of Christianity to work and social relationships, guidance in prayer and Bible reading, and the development of an ability to think theologically. For some, at this stage, it may involve a specific call to the ministry of the church, with further theological and pastoral training.

This second aspect of Christian education has usually been regarded as the work of the churches. But the first aim was fulfilled, at least in theory, by ordinary schooling. The school provided the atmosphere and ethos of the Christian life, centred on daily worship and backed by periods of specific Christian instruction. Even in the sixties, when there were so many changes in education and religion, the underlying theory remained the same. The aim of education in general, and RE in particular, was an encounter with Christ. It was not important whether or not the child realized this at the time. The hope was that he would leave school imbued with Christian values that would hold him in good stead in time of need. Non-Christian teachers in general accepted the approach on the grounds that it ensured a ground in basic moral principles.

But in the present situation it is clear that the first aim of Christian education can no longer be fulfilled in the county school. It is not the school's job to provide a Christian atmosphere, still less to organize itself on the assumption that human wholeness is crowned by a relationship with Christ. The first aim of Christian education falls back on the churches. This has important implications for all individual Christians working in education, and for the church schools.

At the end of the last century, the church schools were maintained in existence to allow for denominational teaching. This was in acknowledgement of the principle, frequently invoked by the Roman Catholic church, that parents have an inalienable right to have their children educated according to their own philosophy and way of life. The Catholic school is seen as: 'Part of the saving mission of the church, especially for education in the faith.'[2] Here, in the church school, is a way of ensuring that the Christian ideal of wholeness in Christ is translated into educational practice:

'She [the church] establishes her own schools because she considers them as a privileged means of promoting the formation of the whole man, since the school is a centre in which a specific concept of the world, of man, and of history is conveyed.'[3] Against accusations that the denominational school leads to a narrow perspective in education it is argued that a specific education fits children better to make a specific contribution to society as a whole. One Jewish headmaster explained that: 'Jewish schools impregnate children with the ideals and culture of their religion, in order that they can be better fitted . . . to make a specific and unique contribution to the mosaic of civilization.'[4]

It is clear that the rights of Roman Catholic and Jewish schools to exist is connected with the rights of any sizeable minority to preserve and pass on its own traditions and values.

The Anglican schools, however, are in a very much more ambiguous position. The Church of England is the established church, it is the church of Queen and state. The Church of England schools set up by the voluntary societies offered education for all. The Tractarians, who set in motion the Catholic movement within the Church of England, argued that the church should make itself completely responsible for the educational system, without assistance from the state. This never happened. But it points to the fact that the sense in which the Church of England is 'established' is, in some ways, very curious. For, it could be argued, if the Church of England *is* established it should have no need of its own schools. The state schools would promote the church's teaching.

But even as early as 1870 it was clear that the teaching given in county schools was to be non-denominational. Church of England schools, like the other voluntary schools, continued under the provision for denominational teaching. This has led some people to wonder why it is that Anglicans still assume a responsibility for all children, on a local, and not denominational basis. There are many small areas where the Anglican school is the neighbourhood school, there simply is no alternative. This is a reflection of the very peculiar role of the Church of England in English life. Everyone lives in an Anglican parish and has the right to ask for baptism. The church buries thousands of people who have never been inside an Anglican church. 'Establishment' in practice seems to mean that the state requires certain functions to be performed by the church, but the church does not get much in the way of privileged treatment from the state. The education issue shows this particularly clearly. It is not surprising that the Church of England's attitude towards its own schools is complex and muddled. In one area a Church of England school might provide a denominational alternative to a county school, in another it would be the local school with responsibility for all-comers.

There are strong arguments against the present system of maintaining separate schools. One argument which weighs heavily with some Christians is that church schools are prevented from giving a church-based education because they are not part of the life of the ordinary church community. The separation between school and parish is maintained by the 1944 Act. No school has a right to require children to take part in Sunday worship. There are also limits on the use of church buildings by church schools. Many church schools exist in an ecclesiastical vacuum. The teachers take no part in the worship of the local church, and the head teacher has little contact with local clergy. Whatever such schools are, they are certainly not the embodiment of the Christian community in education. The artificiality of the situation sometimes affects the children, as in the case of the child at a Roman Catholic school who said: 'I don't like school masses because there are no babies crying and no old women rattling their rosaries.'[5]

Many Christians are more worried by the fact that church schools are cut off from the rest of the educational system. They argue that Christian teachers should be scattered throughout the system as a whole, bringing Christian values to bear in the work of the secular community. There is a danger that too many Christians will be attracted to work in church schools and will leave the church without witness elsewhere. Against this it is frequently argued that for the church to have the right to speak on general educational issues it must have experience of the broad administrative and social issues which apply to the whole of education. The only way for the church to maintain this experience is through its own schools.

Another objection is felt by Christians who argue that it is the church's function to 'incarnate' itself in society, and not to stand apart as a separate culture: 'What we can do at present is to work towards the development of a common language – to begin to build up that linguistic community between church and world which has been absent for so long.'[6] It is clearly one of the functions of education to attempt to build up common language within the community. The church may be failing most radically in its mission to the whole of society precisely by trying to stay separate. Against this it is argued that there is something dishonest about the Christian trying to 'influence' the secular culture in terms that are not openly religious. If the educational system has abandoned its previous Christian philosophy, then it is the task of Christians to make their own philosophy as clear and coherent as possible, so that it can be seen for the alternative that it is.

Some Christian families prefer to send their children to church schools because they feel it imposes a strain on children to go between a home and school that profess different values. For Christian parents, the argument goes, the school run by the church is justified because it maintains a unity between the values taught at home and the values affirmed at school. If this argument is sound, then Christians who support church schools should be vocal in their support for those other communities who want their own schools, the Muslims, and in some areas the Sikhs. It is a far greater cultural strain for a Pakistani child to go from a devout home to the neutral/agnostic English school, than for a Christian.

On the other hand it is clear that there is real educational value in children from different backgrounds being educated together. Most educationists attack the principle of separate education specifically on these grounds. They also point out that the original aim of the denominational schools was to give denominational teaching – in other words to teach doctrine. It was over doctrine that the churches were divided, and separate schools gave the churches the freedom to pass on their individual teachings. Yet it is now generally thought that doctrine cannot be communicated effectively to young children. So the original reason for having denominational schools is no longer thought valid, at least at primary level. Today, many church schools do not attempt to teach doctrine as such. It is likely that there are Roman Catholic infant schools which differ very little from their Anglican equivalents. Neither will make much attempt to teach the formulas of the catechism, both will be influenced by modern educational method. The ways in which they attempt to teach the beginnings of Christian faith and worship may well be similar. The role of the church schools has changed. They are no longer schools for promoting the doctrines of the different churches. Yet it is difficult to be clear as to what their role really is today.

This is particularly true of the Anglican schools. It is very difficult to have a clear cut policy about the role of the church school when it is the only school in an area, and in actual fact has a responsibility for the education of all the children who happen to live there. Schools in this position often do little to distinguish themselves from county schools. They will teach the same kind of RE and adopt an 'open-ended' approach to school worship. If there is any difference it may be in the fact that some of the staff try to provide a 'Christian' atmosphere in the school. But then, so do many Christian teachers in other schools. It should not be assumed that all the teachers in these schools will be committed Anglicans, or even Christians at all. A broad sympathy with the supposed Christian aims of the school may be required, but that is all. Even the head teacher is more likely to be appointed on the grounds of his educational qualifications rather than his commitment to the Church of England. This may seem perfectly fair and appropriate, yet the very existence of these schools requires a financial and moral commitment of the churches for which, crudely, they see very little return. The churches are doing the state's job — perfectly adequately, no doubt, and in some cases, rather better than the state. This raises another problem. Where there is a choice of schools it is sometimes, though by no means always, the case that church schools actually offer a better education. This may be because they are smaller, it may be because they have accumulated a tradition of solid, caring teaching, it may be because they happen to attract more educated teachers. The church schools have the right to give preference to committed church families. It is not an unknown occurrence for parents, anxious that their children should get the best education available, to move into the school's area and start attending the local church in order to secure a place at the school of their choice. Such parents may also feel that the church school represents values of tradition and

T.G. — E

morality which are lacking in other schools; the church school will make sure the children know how to read and write and spell and count; a 'nicer class' of children go to the church school; the church school will provide discipline that other schools do not and the parents cannot; the church school will lay a firm foundation of belief and conduct, which other schools cannot and the parents do not know how to do.

The problem for the churches is whether they should be party to this kind of one-up-man-ship in education. In some areas the church school spells privilege, not the privilege of an education that is paid for out of the parents' pockets, but privilege based, ironically, on excellence and tradition. Parents send their children to these church schools, not because they want them to grow up as Christians, but because they want them to do better than their neighbours. This is very human and understandable, but isn't it a lurking reminder of the old triumphalism of the church? The existence of these schools requires a continuing commitment on the part of the churches, one which looks more like a commitment to preserving the status quo than to preaching and teaching the Gospel of Christ.

Yet it is also true that there are Church of England schools which use their own privileges for the benefit of the wider community. It may be that a headmaster, acting on Christian principles, takes into his school a larger proportion of immigrant children than actually live in the school's area. He is using the church school's right to recruit pupils from outside its catchment area to ease the problem of the numbers of immigrant children in another area. This is obviously socially and educationally useful. The problem is that it may involve the churches in taking on responsibilities which, in the end, they are unable to fulfil. To do the state's job better than the state in one small area, does not actually impel the state to provide better facilities, it merely provides a further drag on the church's resources.

These problems apply most acutely to Anglican schools because of their ambiguous position, but to some degree they affect other denominational schools as well. An even more complex issue is the church's involvement with the public schools. Twenty per cent of our public schools are connected with or run by the churches in one way or another. Many others are linked to the church through tradition. Two Archbishops of Canterbury in this century have been public school headmasters. There are schools run by religious orders which are attached to convents and monasteries. Stoneyhurst and Downside are famous examples. There are also a number of convent-run girls' boarding schools. There are Choir Schools attached to some of the great cathedrals and chapels. Some of them, like King's College School in Cambridge, offer fee-paying preparatory education to boys other than those who sing in the choir. Then there are the schools which, while not run by the churches themselves, were founded in order to provide a Christian education in close connection with the churches. Dr Arnold made the school chapel the centre of the life of Rugby, to which he was appointed as headmaster in 1928. His intention seems to have been to produce Christians, gentlemen and scholars, and roughly in that order. Nathaniel Woodward regarded his schools as a mission to the middle classes. Eton has no less than two chapels and four school chaplains. The churches' investment of time and manpower, if not directly of money, in the public school system is enormous.

The public schools, being independent, are not bound to offer religious education or a daily act of worship. They are outside the provisions of the 1944 Act. At the same time they are not bound to offer the right of withdrawal from RE or school worship. Many schools appoint a full-time chaplain who is responsible for RE teaching and for organizing the worship of the chapel. In many prep schools, at least until recently, RE was a compulsory subject for Common Entrance, and the syllabus was strictly Bible-based.

Most public schools are boarding schools. They function as communities in a much fuller way than day schools. This means that there are more opportunities for communal religion. There can be worship on Sunday as well as weekday services. There are also opportunities for less formal gatherings for prayer, Bible study and communion. These schools are free to regard themselves as Christian communities as far as they wish to. Some Roman Catholic schools exercise this freedom by being 'closed' – that is they will only admit children of committed Catholic parents. Others seek to provide a Christian education for all who can afford to come. In the words of one Roman Catholic headmistress who ran an independent convent school: 'An education that gives all its pupils an opportunity of coming to terms with their environment, of developing fully their powers and possibilities, of encountering the faith which is their heritage. All children are entitled to this last, and it is, in fact, often the non-Catholics who are most grateful for what they receive at school.'[7] This was from a school where just half the girls were Roman Catholics. It was a school that attracted non-Catholic parents because of its high academic standards, its firm Christian philosophy of education and its non-proselytizing attitude to those of other denominations. Non-Catholics were encouraged to involve themselves in the life of their own churches and to seek confirmation or its equivalent. There was joint RE throughout the school except for one period a week of denominational teaching. In the upper part of the school even this one period was done away with since it was the policy of the school that Catholics and non-Catholics should know something of each others' beliefs. In the sixth form philosophy came into the timetable: 'We also include discussion on the existentialists, such general topics as freedom, conscience and authority, because [the pupils] are conditioned nowadays to highly inadequate notions of freedom and conscience, and a thorough examination of these almost unconscious assumptions is very valuable.'[8]

Here the religious school is taking the secular ideology of education head on. These nuns have no qualms about teaching Augustine and Aquinas at sixth form level. They are also prepared to engage in controversial and critical issues. A school like this does not primarily intend to make converts. But a number of people from non-Catholic backgrounds do embrace Catholicism as a result of a Catholic schooling.

In the Anglican public schools religion was and is an accepted part of the day to day life of the school. Until quite recently mass confirmation was the norm and *not* to be confirmed was considered odd. There was no in-consistency between the corporate religion of chapel and the private scruples of adolescents and masters who took part in it, as Evelyn Waugh recalls describing his days at Lancing: 'Adolescent doubts are very tedious to the mature; I was genially assured that it was quite in order for an atheist to act as sacristan.'[9] Sunday worship, of course, was compulsory, and often the very junior boys had to go more often than the seniors. Chaplains were on the teaching staff and often taught subjects other than religion. It is easy to see how, in a school like this, religion was almost a tool of discipline, reinforcing the hierarchies of the school. Life was bound by the bell, ringing for chapel, classes, break, classes, lunch.

The headmaster of Eton still regards the school chapel as the centre of the school, and addresses the parents there at the beginning of the school year. Yet attitudes to religion are changing within the public schools. Many have abandoned mass confirmation. Confirmation classes are usually separated now from the rest of RE. Some schools make an attempt to teach world religions, though it is clear that ordained clergy of the Church of England are hardly the best qualified teachers to do this. As far as worship goes there is more emphasis on flexibility and experiment. At Eton, morning chapel is compulsory for the first few years. It takes the form of a fairly traditional act of Christian worship with a hymn, a reading, prayers, and perhaps a short address by one of the chaplains. Then for a year boys attend a much less-structured assembly which does not necessarily include worship. There may be a talk or a presentation on some social or moral issue, and music from tapes and records. In the sixth form boys are free to choose between a formal service in the large chapel, with traditional music and prayers, and a less formal assembly with less directly religious content.

These changes seem to have come out of the conviction that even a school community which regards itself as Christian cannot compel worship or commitment. There has to be an element of choice and some experience of different forms. For most children this is guaranteed because they live out of school and are confronted with choices by the pluralistic nature of modern society. But a public boarding school is in a different position. There is no doubt that Eton still regards itself as a Christian community, though some would claim that this is manifested in terms of its structure as a caring, supportive community rather than in its formal adherence to Anglican doctrine and practice.

It is not clear yet how the religious life of the public schools has been affected by the increasing number of non-Christian pupils from abroad who come to England to be educated. For a long time there has been a small proportion of children from India and the Arab world who have gone through the English public school system as a preliminary to study at Oxford or Cambridge. But now this trend is increasing, and with the growing power and influence of the Arab oil states wealthy Muslims seek education for their children in the English public schools. They are among the very few who can afford it.

This raises what for many is the greatest problem over

the churches' involvement with the public schools. The first public schools were schools for the poor. Eton itself catered originally for the less well-off, who could not afford the luxury of grammar school education. The schools started by teaching orders of monks and nuns offered cheap education for those who otherwise could not have afforded it. Now these schools are frequently criticized for being 'bastions of privilege'. The fees are way beyond the reach of all but the most wealthy. The public schools are accused of perpetuating class divisions, and of preparing pupils to regard themselves as an intellectual and social elite.

The Durham report discussed the issue of religion and the public schools at length and concluded that there was too high a proportion of ordained men working in them. The church in education cares more about its ministry to the rich than to the poor if numbers are anything to go by. It is also true, of course, that many schools have bishops as governors; these are regularly invited to preach and take confirmations.

Many Christians are questioning the churches' involvement in the public schools on theological grounds. The schools started as a service to the poor. Some teaching orders are withdrawing from the public school system and diverting their attention to inner city areas. They are being recruited into the county school system or strengthening the staff of voluntary schools.

Some Christians working within the public school system argue that the children of the rich have as much right to Christian education as anyone else. The public schools can justify themselves as 'citadels of excellence' rather than 'bastions of privilege'. The public schools are right to offer a Christian education to those who will bear power and responsibility in the future. Christian education ensures that the ideals of service and responsibility are set before the pupils. The Christian is committed to excellence, to bring out what is highest and best

in man. There is, therefore, no inconsistency between
Christian commitment and involvement in the public
school system. Indeed, when the state system has abandoned the Christian basis of education the public schools
remain as pockets of Christian witness and community.

Against this, Christians point to the teachings of the Old
Testament prophets on the demand for social justice.
Christians should be critical of an educational system that
is socially divisive. Jesus, like the prophets, shows that
God is biased in favour of the poor and underprivileged:
'In the gospels Jesus is biased toward the left: he takes
his place with those who are certainly not the King's
men . . . he takes sides apparently because God has taken
sides: and to the Magnificat he adds the Beatitudes. God
is biased in favour of the poor and the meek; the rich
and the powerful – no matter what the church has taught
– have no part in God's kingdom.'[10]

Against this there are those who argue that the church
has in recent years been too uncritical in its acceptance
of socialist ideology, and that in confusing the gospel
with socialism it is giving in to the spirit of the age.

It is impossible to separate out the religious and
political arguments about the churches and the public
schools. It is ironic that at a time when the church is
having to strip itself of privileges and certainty in other
areas of education, public school religion should apparently be flourishing, and the ideals of Christian education,
on the whole, remain intact. Public school religion is civic
religion at its best. It is the religion of Christendom, but
it is Christendom that still has some life in it, and because
there is life in it, it can breed criticism and prophecy.
This is certainly what is happening when a teaching order
of nuns gives up its independent convent school and goes
to teach in the inner city. It may also happen when, in
spite of the anomaly of the public schools in our educational system, the Christian faith is passed down to a new
generation in the context of a humble and caring com-

munity. Many of the schools do not 'belong' to the churches. The churches have no financial commitment to the schools. The association is based on voluntary goodwill. There is, therefore, the possibility for the church to be an educator in its role as servant – in spite of the media image of hearty, cricket-playing chaplains and portly bishops arriving in large cars to conduct the annual confirmation. The independence of the public schools is the basis of their right to conduct themselves as Christian communities. But do the non-independent voluntary religious schools have that right in today's society?

The only convincing argument begins from the attitude frequently put forward by secularists and humanists who have long been opposed in principle to the idea of separate education. They assume that separate education means indoctrination, which is never fair or justified. They point to the fact that separate education is politically divisive. In Northern Ireland the separation between the county schools, which are the pastoral concern of the Church of Ireland and the Presbyterian church, and the Roman Catholic education system has aggravated hostility and prejudice in the community. The humanists declare that education should prepare children for living in an open society. Diversity of viewpoint and mutual tolerance and respect are essential for building up a truly human community. Most Christians accept the humanist view of community, and many accept the argument that separate education is against the interests of the open society. Most Jewish parents in this country, and an increasing number of Sikhs and Muslims, have no desire for their children to be educated separately. They feel that religion should be passed on in the home. To take this point of view does not mean that one shares the humanists' attack on religion. But it does mean inevitably that religion comes to be seen as a private matter. It may be the source of inspiration for social or political action, but it can have no embodiment in society. It also means an acceptance of cultural

and religious relativism, which, it could be argued, is a
denial of a certain sort of human freedom. In an official
statement 'The Catholic School' the Sacred Congregation
for Catholic Education declares: 'Cultural pluralism . . .
leads the church to reaffirm her mission of education . . .
Her children then will be capable both of resisting the
debilitating influence of relativism and of living up to the
demands made upon them by their baptism . . . for this
reason the church is prompted to mobilize her educational
resources in the face of the materialism, pragmatism and
technocracy of today's society.'[11]

This should not be interpreted as an attempt by the
church to take over the educational system. Its own
claim is founded on an *acceptance* of pluralism: 'The
church upholds the principle of a plurality of school
systems in order to safeguard her objectives in the face of
cultural pluralism.'[12] The church's objectives here are not
to impose itself in the place of secular culture, but to
ensure that, within the church, the tradition and reality
of Catholic life is handed down. The fact that sizeable
groups still need to opt out of the secular system reveals
the major flaw in the humanists' argument: 'Education
for a participant democracy implies a comprehensive
pattern of education. Children should not be segregated
according to their race, colour, creed, sex, social position,
academic powers or any other such arbitrary criteria.
Public schools and direct grant schools (voluntary religious
schools are not mentioned, but the argument must ulti-
mately include them) should be absorbed into a secular
school system. Within this framework, variety, experiment and research should be encouraged.'[13] Excluded
from this framework, of course, would be the attempt
for a school to live as a Christian community or to promote an Islamic life-style.

The humanist proposal also assumes that: 'the attain-
ment of autonomy in moral understanding by all children
becomes the basis of personal life and social order.'[14] The

humanists offer their plan of education for the open society as a blueprint for the future. They feel its ideals still need to be implemented. Yet it is clear that their attitudes are shared by most of today's educationists. It is a philosophy which many Christians have come to share. John Hull, for example, welcomes the secularization of education, religious education in particular. As we have already seen, he allows that education in this country is the child of Christianity, but sets out to show how it has outgrown its Christian origins. He goes on to argue that there is an inevitable tension between Christian faith and education. Education requires an attitude of neutrality and openness, and the acceptance of pluralism. Education helps a child to make critical judgements. Education is not authoritarian. Education enables the child to choose whether or not to be religiously committed: 'What the result of this intention will actually be for the welfare and prosperity of the various faiths is not education's concern, for education has no aim other than further learning.'[15]

Hull's stress on education as a 'neutral' tool of growth and on the autonomy of the individual in making religious, and presumably moral, choices, is close to the humanist view. The problem with this view is that its proponents do not recognize that it is a *view*, only a view, a philosophy in its own right. Education is not neutral. It is, inevitably, an initiation into a particular set of values and attitudes. John Hull would agree with this to some extent, but he would claim that aims in education are guided by our view of man. Yet the view of man proposed by the humanists is by no means identical to the view of man proposed by Christian theology. Humanist man is alone in the universe. He is morally autonomous. The purpose of his life is human happiness, which is to be achieved through human means alone. He is capable of finding meaning because his basic characteristics are sympathy with his fellow human-beings, and reason. These characteristics have developed through evolution. Christian man is incomplete man. He is made with a God-shaped gap, and can only be fulfilled in God. God is the source of his being, and so without God he is frustrated and unfulfilled. Man has the potential for goodness, sympathy and reason, but finds that the potential is marred by selfishness and greed. There is certainly common ground between the Christian and the humanist view of man. But from the Christian point of view the humanist picture is too narrow. Education for the Christian cannot in the end involve an attitude of neutrality towards the transcendent dimension. For the Christian faith is not an arbitrary choice, it is the key that makes sense of the whole of reality. So for the Muslim and the Jew. To regard education as a neutral tool of human growth is to accept the humanist philosophy of man. It is to regard faith as purely a private matter, an optional extra, a quirk of psychology by which some earth-bound individuals occasionally have a glimpse of heaven.

If it is the case that the humanist perspective, far from being neutral as it claims, is in fact a particular and narrowing view of man, and if it is true that this perspective forms the basis of most current educational theory, accepted as it is uncritically by humanists and non-humanists alike, then the case for religious schools can proceed on the basic grounds of human freedom. A religious school should provide a genuine criticism and alternative to prevailing assumptions. This criticism is valuable and necessary in any truly 'open' society. The religious school, be it Christian, Jewish or Muslim, should stand for the view that religion and morality are not merely private choices. The religious school should be a protest against the assumption that private life and public life are separate. Some religious schools do offer just this kind of critical alternative in our own system. Many do not, and it is significant that some Christian educationists are opposed to the idea that they should do so: 'What

Christians need to be sensitive to is the extent to which there is a continuing acceptance of the Christian "concept of man" as forming the groundwork of all our educational endeavours. *Only if the Christian churches were convinced that this had finally been abandoned* in our national educational system would they be justified in calling for retrenchment within the walls of our existing church schools.'[16] Yet it is difficult to imagine how the Christian churches would ever be able to assess precisely the moment at which the Christian concept of man ceased to be the groundwork for the state's educational endeavours. To many it will seem that the concept has been eroded by degrees over many years, so that liberal-minded Christians, influenced by secularist assumptions, are hardly aware that it is absent.

The churches, however, should look carefully at their existing schools and ask how far they are fulfilling their role as an alternative to the state schools. The church schools which, under the 1944 Act, opted for controlled status have no real opportunity to offer a Christian education. Yet the church still owns the buildings, and from the public's point of view, are involved in the teaching and governing. Of the aided schools those that are the only available schools in the neighbourhood are doing little more than a charitable job on behalf of the state. Others seem by their very excellence to be perpetuating privilege in education. This may not be a reason for closing them, but it may be a reason for the church to consider handing them over to the state. It is a question of priorities.

One encouraging development in recent years has been the start of a number of ecumenical church schools where Catholics and Anglicans, and Anglicans and Non-Conformists are jointly responsible for a new kind of church school. This might seem an ironic turn-about in the light of the fact that the original justification for church schools was that they were denominational. But there is

some evidence that the idea of a united Christian school
is not such a bolt out of the blue.

In 1788 the Reverend Joseph Berrington, a Roman
Catholic priest, was arguing for the extension of church-
run education and pleaded: 'That we for once forget that
we are Church of England men, Presbyterians, Baptists,
Roman Catholics or Quakers.'[17] His views at the time
were certainly unusual, but they were not condemned.
However, in 1852 the Roman Catholic church embarked
on its own strictly separatist policy in England when the
First Westminster Synod called for each congregation to
have its own schools, one for each sex. Cardinal Manning
expressed his fear that Catholic children would be diverted
from the true faith if they were educated in non-Catholic
schools. The Catholic ideal became that: 'Every Catholic
child from a Catholic home to be taught by Catholic
teachers in a Catholic school.' But the ideal has never
been realized, and the majority of Catholic children have
had at least part of their education in non-Catholic schools.
Vatican statements, however, have assumed that parents
are under a religious obligation to try and educate their
children in Catholic schools.

There is division among Catholics today on the future
of Catholic education. Many still feel that the separate
school is a vital factor in the upbringing of their children.
Others are less certain, and argue that separate schools
lead to a narrow inwardness which is opposed to Christian
freedom. Yet others look to the non-denominational
Christian school as a sign of hope for the future, and,
following in the footsteps of Father Berrington declare
that: 'Any current experiments in sharing Christian
schools with other denominations would be well within
our educational tradition and would be fully consonant
with those principles of loyalty to the church and to the
faith for which (our) forefathers made so many sacrifices.'[18]

St Bede's Comprehensive School in Redhill was formed
by bringing together the Bishop Simpson Comprehensive

(Anglican) and the smaller St Joseph's Roman Catholic School. The two headmistresses presented a joint statement to their governors: 'The condition of society at present calls for a clear and convincing witness of Christian solidarity in the face of the challenge from humanists, the general indifference to moral issues and the apathy of nominal Christians who are uncommitted to the Christian way of life.'[19]

After much heartsearching on the part of the governors and staff, and much public discussion, the joint school was formed. It now caters for eleven hundred children. The Anglican headmistress is head of the joint school and the Roman Catholic headmistress acts as her deputy. Visitors report a high standard of academic life and a 'Christian' atmosphere of warmth and friendliness. From the start it was intended that there should be no watering down of denominational beliefs: 'Each tradition would bring its own richness to the common study of the Christian faith in mutual respect.' Some of the RE classes are shared, some are denominational. There is a single, united act of daily worship. There is a lunchtime mass for the Catholics and an after school prayer-meeting. There is no chapel, but two chaplains, an Anglican and a Roman Catholic.

It is too early yet to assess the effectiveness of this new kind of Christian school. There have been criticisms of St Bede's from some Catholics who feel that the distinctive quality of Catholic education has been lost. On the other hand it shows that an ecumenical school is a very different proposition from the supposed Christian county schools of between the wars. The ecumenical school does not water down denominational differences, nor does it refuse the issues of doctrine. It may be here that the churches are able to begin to offer a credible alternative within the school system.

But what is the criterion of success for a church school? There is some evidence that those educated in church schools do not necessarily remain attached to a church in any greater numbers than those who have been educated in secular schools. Home background seems to make the biggest difference to later patterns of churchgoing.

Is it success if a child from a Roman Catholic school knows how to cross himself and pray even though, as an adult, he never goes to mass? Is it success if children grow up rejecting Christian dogma and piety and yet retaining a sense of the sacred in human life, and a dedication to the ideals of service and love? Could not these ideals be taught satisfactorily within a secular context? There is no clear-cut answer to these questions. In the end the church's commitment to education is an act of faith. It is made in the belief that it is better that there should be the opportunity for children to grow up within a Christian community than that they should be denied that opportunity, and that the generally unpopular view that man is incomplete without God needs institutional embodiment.

But there is also a need, and perhaps a great need, for Christian witness within the state system of education. This poses a real dilemma for Christian teachers. They may well be offered the choice at some stage in their career between teaching in a small rewarding community of a Christian school, whether it is a public school or a voluntary school, or trying the rough and tumble and frustration of a large secular comprehensive. For some Christians it will appear as a choice between an easy option and a difficult one. But it is not always so clear-cut in practice. The Christian socialist working in a public school faces a particular set of problems, the Christian who believes in discipline and tradition in an unruly comprehensive faces another. Some may find themselves in a voluntary church school which is doing nothing but perpetuating religious and social conservatism, others may find themselves in a happy successful secular school where there appears to be no need for the Christian gospel.

The Christian attachment is to the Kingdom of God, and not to any status quo, whether that of the public schools, of liberal Humanism, or of modern socialist or conservative politics. This realization should make Christians in all branches of education open and critical, wary of the political clichés of right and left which pretend to have the force of moral or religious tradition. The Christian teacher today must start from the realization that he is in a minority, though there may be others willing to share the Christian perspective on specific issues. But to hold the view that man is incomplete without God and that the purpose of the human quest is God himself, marks the Christian in society both publicly and privately. One thing he will retain from the past is the sense of personal vocation. Vocation has always been part of the meaning of being a Christian. In Christian society, in the community that gives thanks in the Eucharist, each individual had his role and function ordained by God. The idea of vocation is linked to the idea of mutual service and love. The leader is the one who serves, the strong protect and care for the weak. We have seen how, whenever Christendom becomes established as a political order, it loses its vision of the kingdom, and adopts a worldly triumphalism, glorying in the power of here and now. And yet something of the sense of personal vocation and mutual fellowship lives on. Until recently this was most notable in medicine and teaching. Many who entered these professions, even if they rejected Christian faith, had a strong personal sense of service, a commitment to the weak and the poor, and an acceptance of long hours and inconveniences as the price for the sense of personal fulfilment in work. Now, in the secular world, these ideals are widely regarded as unrealistic. Teaching and nursing are jobs like anything else. It is argued that talk of vocation and service was a sham for covering the disgrace of low pay and poor working conditions. Now there is no doubt some truth in this, and the

Christian teacher may well reflect that outside of a Christian understanding of life the ideals of service and fellowship do look fairly unrealistic. We can see in this century how the ideals outlasted the Christian faith which inspired them by a few years and no more. So much for the argument that Christian behaviour can be separated from Christian belief. But the Christian teacher brings to his work a sense of vocation which is rooted in belief. The nature of his commitment is different, and he will probably have to suffer for it. So his witness in the secular school could be one not so much of speech as of service, not of giving away his faith, but giving away himself in a way that perhaps few teachers in our secular schools are free enough to do.

NOTES

1. *Report of Joint Study Commission on Education*, presented to the Fourth Assembly of the World Council of Churches in 1968. Quoted in *The Fourth 'R'*, p. 205
2. *The Catholic School*: The Sacred Congregation for Catholic Education, Rome, 1977, Catholic Truth Society, p. 7
3. Ibid. p. 7
4. *Looking Forward to the Seventies*: Edward Conway, p. 292-4. Quoted in *The Fourth 'R'*, p. 208
5. 'Religious Education and The Sixth Form': Hamish Swanston in *Religious Education*, p. 69
6. *The New Left Church*: Terry Eagleton, Sheed and Ward 1966, p. 180
7. 'The Open Religious School': Sister Catherine Appleby in *Religious Education*, p. 91
8. Ibid. p. 92
9. *A Little Learning*: Evelyn Waugh, Sidgwick & Jackson 1973, p. 140
10. *A Reader in Political Theology*: edited by Alistair Kee, SCMP 1974, p. XI
11. *The Catholic School*: p. 12
12. Ibid.

13. *Education for the Open Society*, British Humanist Association, p. 5

14. Ibid.

15. *School Worship – an Obituary* : p. 85

16. *The Christian in Education* : Colin Alves, SCMP 1972, p. 98

17. 'Roman Catholic Educational Policy' : Michael Gaine in *Religious Education*, p. 147

18. Ibid. p. 163

19. As reported in *The Catholic Herald*

CHAPTER SIX

God, Science and Society

Education involves passing on a set of values from one generation to another. School syllabuses and timetables should tell us something about the society we live in, the assumptions it makes, its priorities and hopes. The latest RE syllabuses, as we have seen, tend to go in two different directions. First, they value 'scientific method' – regarding religion as a social phenomenon which can be analysed, categorized and evaluated by applying the right criteria. Second, they try to open up personal, social and moral issues for free and informed discussion, where the stress is on the individual's experience and his search for meaning.

What do the new syllabuses tell us about the society we live in and its attitude to religion? The picture is confused. On the one hand the syllabuses assume we are living in a 'pluralist' society, a society, in other words, made up of people of a variety of religious beliefs and different cultural backgrounds. At the same time, the syllabuses reflect a society that is fundamentally secular; it has no religious centre, no shared perception, no common vision about the nature of man and his place in the universe. Religion, insofar as it has any meaning, can only have private meanings in such a society. Because we live in this society we know that both the pluralist and the secular descriptions are correct. We also know that the new syllabuses represent a conscious break with the 'Christian' past; they bring no comfort to that large number of parents and teachers who deplore the abandonment of 'our Christian heritage'. The syllabuses also tell us that the test of true secularity is the adoption of scientific method'.

It is a cliché today to assert that we live in a science-based culture. It is also still widely felt that science and religion are at war with each other, and that science has the upper hand. Most RE teachers will be familiar with pupils who assume that science has disproved religion, that religion is a lot of myths, fables and fairy stories, whereas science produces hard facts. The General Synod Board of Education survey confirms how widespread this view is and speaks of: 'an uncritical acceptance of a vocabulary of natural science'[1] by the young people who took part in the survey. It is certainly uncritical. It is not uncommon to find these 'scientifically-minded' young people bowled over by the pseudo-scientific 'explanations' of religious phenomena like Von Daniken's *Chariot of the Gods*. Von Daniken's theories have been publicly discredited by historians and archaeologists, but his blend of fantasy and scientific jargon make his theories irresistible to those for whom 'science' has become the chief authority in matters of belief: 'Instead of religion our young people have a mild form of science-fiction.'[2]

Along with this blind attachment to science goes an unquestioning individualism. Beliefs about religion are private and personal. They have nothing to do with anyone else. They do not need to be explained or talked through, and they are not open to anyone else's criticism or disproof. The survey concludes that what has happened to the beliefs of young people is related to an all-dominating advance in the jargon of rationality, science and individualism. In contrast, going alongside this cerebral language is a private emotional language of experience and belief. The new syllabuses, instead of offering a critique of this position in fact seem to adopt and confirm it. True, their use of scientific criteria is more sophisticated, but it is just as blind. They may be concerned to make inner experience articulate, but they are just as convinced that it is essentially private and personal.

Yet how far is the scientific paradigm appropriate to the study of religion? The question is elusive because science itself is problematic. In the years of bitter conflict between the church and science, the sciences were proceeding on the basis that matter is explicable without reference to God. From the church's point of view this was a kind of blasphemy. But it was not really blasphemy. The churches had to learn, painfully, to give up their domination of human culture and thought, and to accept the idea that created reality was open to observation and experiment. The debate left a problem of location. If scientific study did not reveal God, where was he? Newton 'located' God in absolute space and time, outside the created order. He was working with the concept of the universe as a giant machine, running on regular and unchangeable laws which were constituted by God at the beginning. The task of science was to discover these laws by experiment and analysis, and thus discover how the machine works.

This way of acquiring knowledge about the universe seemed so certain and so objective that 'scientific method' was adopted in other disciplines as well. Of course it was true that history and geography and theology had all proceeded by collecting and analysing evidence, but now scientific method was applied to the study of man in a more total and far-reaching way. Marx assumes that his view of man is 'scientific' and his doctrine of dialectical materialism can be read off the face of history by anyone able to understand the evidence. The humanists of the last century believed that it was the theory of evolution that had provided them with their 'scientific' picture of man. Evolution proved that man was no fallen angel created for glory, but a random development of natural processes which still awaited the fulfilment of its potential. God was not necessary for the hypothesis of humanists or Marxists, and indeed, they understood religion as a misinterpretation by man of his predicament, brought about by his loneliness and fear.

'Science' by this stage had become much more than a method. It had become a popular philosophy, the basis of a new culture. School children today regard science as authoritative. A scientist may be proved wrong, but he can only be proved wrong by another scientist, not by a philosopher or a historian. School children may be bored by science but they accept its authority without question. Religion on the other hand is suspect, bogus and hypocritical.

The churches have responded to the scientific age with various degrees of success. Fundamentalists have continued to assert the primacy of Biblical explanations over scientific ones, as if the Bible and science were really offering rival theories. On the whole though, since the Darwin controversy, the churches have come to assess science more positively. Religion has argued that science needs religion to save it from its own power, and that all human truth comes from God:

'God of concrete, God of steel
God of piston and of wheel
God of pylon, God of steam,
God of girder and of beam,
God of atom, God of mine,
All the world of power is thine.'[8]

We have already seen how some of the RE syllabuses have tried in their advanced courses to make pupils aware that the relation between science and religion can be a positive one.

It is, however, a myth to claim that our culture is scientific. It is a myth in the sense that it is partially true, but that the belief that it is true is stronger than the evidence. For a start the fundamental objectivity of science has been questioned by science itself. The old view of the universe as a perfect self-regulating machine

has broken down since the discovery of relativity an
the quantum theory. That is not to say that the mode
of the universe as a machine has been abandoned; it is a
extremely useful model in most branches of natura
science, but it is only a model and there could be other
It is no longer clear that the language of scientific ratio
ality yields objective truth. At some levels of investigatio
the universe yields results which are unpredictable, an
cannot be determined by the traditional objective method
Some scientists believe that science can only tell us th
truth in the terms of our own presuppositions. If w
choose to see the universe as a machine, then up to
certain point it will appear to behave like a machine. Bu
beyond that point we are in a no man's land. In othe
words although it is widely believed that science ha
access to objective truth, and that there is no real trut
outside scientific truth, scientists themselves are ofte
much more cautious than the public and much more oper
minded about the limitations of scientific method. Th
impact of these changes is still filtering through th
scientific world, it has hardly reached the popular leve
at all. At the same time the sciences have tended t
become more and more specialized, and no generalize
view of what science is about has emerged to replace th
old rather imperialistic view. However, in the socia
sciences and now in religion the old certainties are sti
cherished; here are a set of beliefs, rituals, myths. B
studying them and applying a set of 'objective' criteri
we can analyse these elements and show how they work
Then we will have discovered what religion is.

At the same time philosophy, influenced by science
has tended to opt out of questions of truth and meaning
British philosophy has been dominated by linguisti
philosophy in recent years. This has concentrated o
finding the meanings of statements by considering how
they are used. Out of this approach has come the 'ver
fication principle' which is that the meaning of a state

ment is revealed by the way in which it is shown to be true or false. Exponents of this brand of philosophy argue that religious statements are meaningless because there is no way in which they can be proved true or false. This bleak philosophy has had an important influence. It has filtered through in a general popularized way to the arts and the humanities. Ironically, though, it is increasingly being abandoned by the philosophers who formerly elucidated it.

David Holbrook in *Education, Nihilism and Survival* suggests that the sciences and the philosophy that has grown out of them have presented a reductionist view of man. That is to say that all considerations of man as a moral or spiritual being are regarded as meaningless. All that can be explained of man is the movement of atoms and molecules which constitute his body and his brain processes. Science began with the recognition that certain aspects of man could be studied as objects. It has ended in the dogma that man *is* an object: 'We are subjected continually, not least in the arts, and in the humanities, in education, to a new dogma, a new metaphysics, whose assumptions are nihilistic – there is nothing to believe in, all former values are discredited, life can have no meaning.'[4]

Dr Holbrook continues by pointing out that this dogma rests entirely on the assumption that we live in the universe portrayed by Newton, the universe which is a machine. If all reality is moving matter operated by chance and necessity, then man is without meaning. Much popular drama and film and television start from these nihilistic assumptions. Society is haunted by violence and pornography because it is schizoid. The schizoid personality cannot love or respond to love. It acts violently in a desperate attempt to *feel*, but this attempt is doomed to frustration. Popular scientism has created the schizoid society because it has deprived us of our sense of meaning: 'This has infected education. Outside the school the child and the youth are exposed to a constant stream of films and television programmes whose message is plainly nihilistic. In school he will have to study works which imply that human existence is meaningless, and there is no way that it can be lived with purpose and authenticity.'[5]

Dr Holbrook describes himself as an atheist humanist. His concern is to restore the human dimensions to education, which he feels has been undermined by the false objectivity and reductionism of scientific culture. He is himself committed to the liberal values of open and empirical study, but he castigates his fellow liberals for their naïvety and inability to perceive the current crisis: 'To many liberals the human personality is largely incorruptible. If we leave matters "open" and "uncontrolled" most people will "swim". The imagination must be completely free, and no damage will be done. One may applaud this confidence in human rationality, but it contains a fallacious underestimation of the powers of fanatical immoralists or schizoid manipulators to enlist others in their psychopathology.'[6]

The liberals, according to Dr Holbrook, are colluding with those who produce pornography and glorify violence, in denying that there is a problem. He does not discuss the problem of religious education as such, but it is likely that the new syllabuses would fall within his pattern of crude scientism coupled with individualism. To Dr Holbrook this is to make them bearers of a destructive and reductionist philosophy.

There has, in fact, been some mild re-thinking from religious educationists about trends in RE. Some have blamed the Birmingham syllabus for being too academic. Others have questioned the stance of strict neutrality on issues of the truth and falsehood of the religions. Behind these criticisms is the beginnings of doubt about the scientific approach and how appropriate it is to the study of religions. The problem is that the scientific approach at least claims to be neutral. It was assumed that no one would be able to accuse RE teachers of brain-washing or overt evangelism. Educationists are now coming to see that scientism, which has its basis in an out of date and over-confident view of science, is itself an option and a choice. It is putting over a view of reality every bit as all-embracing as Christianity, and one which, according at least to David Holbrook, is a reflection of negative and schizoid tendencies within society.

But what alternative is there? This is the problem facing religious educationists, teachers and parents in the next decade. For they are being forced to consider the possibility that religion cannot be taught adequately within the context of a purely secular philosophy. To teach religion at all, once the old scientific method has been abandoned, is to acknowledge, implicitly, that religion has value, firstly for the school community, and secondly as a whole. The implications of that are directly counter to the prevailing philosophy of education, but not, I believe, with a wider search for meaning within society as a whole.

Are we then returning to Christianity without the church and to the politics of Christendom? I believe that way is barred, but there are still many who think and hope that the signs are pointing in that direction. So they argue that the values on which our civilization is built are Christian ones and that RE is one of the vehicles for handing these down to the next generation. Only these inherited values can save society from nihilism. Lord Blake argues in *Curriculum Christianity* 'Christianity has been and still is so inextricably entwined with the very roots of our civilization . . . that . . . I would like to argue that without it a child simply cannot begin to comprehend the history of the civilization in which he or she is being educated.'[7]

Lord Blake goes on to suggest that Christianity should be taught by those who think in the Christian tradition,

even if they are not active Christians. These are the
people who are in a position to interpret history correctly.
They are less likely 'to use a lop-sided interpretation of it
to justify and excuse some of the worst tyrannies of our
times'. Lord Blake regards Marxism as the greatest threat
to Christian civilization. The stand that a Christian
society should take against Marxism is a continuation of
the stand taken against Fascism. It is difficult to escape
the impression that Lord Blake regards Christianity
primarily as a civilizing force. It is to be used today as
a political weapon against totalitarian philosophies.
Christianity becomes inseparable from politics. It is the
source of our own civilization and provides the shape for
it. It is expressed in democracy, in capitalism, in the
institutions of Parliament, in the traditions of free speech.
It is not considered necessary, if this view is held, that
vast numbers of people should go to church or believe
that Christianity is true. Indeed, many of those who would
support Lord Blake's argument have no great desire to
become committed Christian believers. But they expect
the church to be open to them. They desire baptism for
their children, they want Christianity to be taught in the
schools as a kind of protection against the forces of darkness which they rightly perceive to be near the surface
of society. Such people do not regard themselves as anything other than Christian, they say they believe in God,
and probably turn to prayer in times of sickness or
trouble. They are distressed when they go to church and
find that the liturgy has changed. They always hope that
the church will be the focus for what is solid and enduring
in a world of bewildering change. Such parents will
support movements for traditional RE. The humanists
claim that these parents have misunderstood traditional
RE and really want their children to get some sort of
moral education. Yet I think it is likely that many parents
need the assurance of transcendence. Even if they are not
sure of their own beliefs, morality without religion sounds

dangerous. To them it means immorality, permissiveness, all the things that can be thought in private but should be condemned when they are spoken in public. So parents worry about their children learning about Humanism and Communism and having sex education classes. These represent an anarchic spirit, a movement of chaos. RE however should be laying a firm foundation of discipline. It does not matter if the beliefs of Christianity are later rejected. Many parents would be more anxious if RE classes *did* provoke their children into regular church-going. One of the reasons why this attitude is so prevalent is that parents have lost confidence in their own ability to educate. They are nervous of the past and of the changes that have come over society. They know that on the whole the media favour the young and attractive; for the media the past is dead. In vain they look to the schools to provide some sense of continuity and tradition. But the schools themselves are looking in the opposite direction. So also are the churches.

Jacques Ellul, a French Protestant writer, is cynical about this half-religious attitude, this yearning for Christendom.[8] He sees it as a perversion of Christianity, paganism in the guise of the gospel. At the same time he feels that the real unquestioned presuppositions of French society are those of atheistic humanism. Most people live as if God did not exist. Politicians, economists, journalists, teachers, even clergy, all proceed on the basis that God does not exist, however much they claim to believe in God in their personal lives. Ellul's vision of an atheist society, which is not so different from the atheist David Holbrook's vision of a nihilistic society, does not exclude the nostalgia for Christendom. Indeed practical atheism and romantic Christianity can exist quite happily side by side in the same person.

The nostalgia for Christendom which we see in the writing of Lord Blake and others is fuelled by the memory of the one period in recent history when Christendom was vindicated, the Second World War. It was an assumption shared by almost everyone that the issue of the war was the struggle of Christian civilization against a new and terrible paganism. During this period many people felt there was more in Christianity than they had realized. When it came to the crunch the war was about two incompatible views of man.

Yet Biblical Christianity holds out no guarantee that a civilization that regards itself as Christian will in fact be one. When the fascist movements were beginning in Europe there were many influential Christians who saw them as a sign of hope for the future. In Germany leading churchmen gave their allegiance to the Nazi cause. Protestant parsons preached of God's judgement against the Jews. Liberal theologians welcomed the new culture, and church groups were formed with the express purpose of building an alliance between Christianity and National Socialism. But as early as 1921 the young Karl Barth had published a commentary on the Epistle to the Romans which questioned the possibility of Christian culture, and raised afresh the question of divine judgement on human society. For some years Barth refused to comment on the rise of Nazism. He taught that it was a purely secular movement and, as such, had no relevance to the Gospel. Later he came vigorously to oppose Nazism, not on ideological grounds, not by invoking 'Christendom', but because he realized that the freedom of the Gospel itself was at stake. His own Confessing Church was forced underground. Barth had realized that Christendom itself posed the greatest threat to Christianity. Christendom meant compromise with the powers of this world. This can take an immense variety of forms from the German Church Movement, to Moral Re-Armament, to certain emerging forms of Christian Marxism. In offering his critique of Christian civilization, Barth has forced the church to reconsider its relationship with the state.

The relationship between Christian faith and culture

has always been ambiguous. Christian faith was not, at the start, a religion for cultured intellectuals. Most of the Athenians who heard Paul's proclamation on Mars Hill reacted with cynicism or cultivated curiosity. Paul himself reminds the church in Corinth of its humble origins: 'Consider your call brethren; not many of you were wise according to worldly standards . . . God chose what is foolish in the world to shame the wise.'[9] The Christian preaching of the cross of Jesus is 'a stumbling block to Jews and folly to the Greeks'. The preaching of the cross did not fit neatly into Judaism or Hellenism. It was a scandal, a contradiction, an obscene joke in dubious religious taste. Paul, as an educated cultured Jew with some awareness of Hellenistic literature and philosophy, realized that the gospel of Christ involved man in a profound crisis. No theologian has expressed this so vividly as Karl Barth: 'The gospel is not a truth among other truths. Rather it sets a question mark against all truths . . . the power of God is not the most exalted of observable forces, nor is it either their sum or their fount. Being completely different it is the KRISIS of all power.'[10] Barth's claim runs counter to much current thinking about the evolution of different religious systems. Trevor Ling, for example, believes that all the great religions are remnants of civilizations. A religion, as he sees it, originates in 'a total view of the world and man's place in it and a total prescription for the ordering of human affairs in all the various dimensions which in the modern world are separated and distinguished from each other as philosophy, politics, economics, ethics, law and so on'.[11] So, for Professor Ling, Christendom was the inevitable expression of Christianity, and represented Christianity at the peak of its flowering. There is less evidence for this point of view in the history of Christianity than there is in the history of some of the other great religions. Islam, for example, was a civilization from the start. There was no question of Muslims buckling down to a minority existence, waiting for the end. Yet this is precisely what the first Christians did. They did not, to start with, seek power within the empire, merely survival.

At the same time the first Christians saw the Gospel as a fulfilment of previous history. In their preaching they used the Old Testament, particularly the Psalms and the prophetic books, to demonstrate that the birth, death and resurrection of Jesus was ordained by God and in accordance with the scriptures.

As the church moved out into the gentile world it faced the same problems with Hellenistic culture. It was still important to show that Christian faith involved a radical break, a change of heart and a response of faith. At the same time the Christian God was not an unknown God. He had declared himself through the history of Israel and the resurrection of Jesus. He was not without witness in the non-Jewish world, the poets and philosophers hinted at him, and a dim reflection of his law was present in the human conscience. Faith in Christ meant that man was no longer subject to the forces of the cosmos. His fate was no longer dictated by the stars. He was free from the influence of demons. He was no longer bound by necessity. The Christians also stood in a critical attitude to the state. Their loyalty was not to any image of God, whether it was a human image or one carved in stone. In spite of this critical independence the church found some of the ideas of Greek philosophy useful in its proclamation of the Gospel. While maintaining the essentially Hebrew vision of the oneness and transcendence of God, they found in Stoic philosophy ideas which helped to make coherent the ideas of God's immanence and of his Logos, or Word, active in creation. Part of this process of translating ideas from one culture to another had been started by Hellenistic Jews, and the Christian church baptized their efforts.

The church's relationship to culture in this period could be described as both critical and free. Christianity was a new beginning which freed men from the limitations of their culture. Yet at the same time God was not without witness within culture itself. For those who have eyes to see there were veiled hints of the Gospel in Roman and Greek literature, in philosophy, and, of course, in the tradition of the Jews.

During the first few centuries the church was pre-occupied with survival and growth. It was necessary to have a public face of apologetic to the world, which would refute charges that Christianity was subversive to the state, and would give an answer to Jewish and Hellenistic critics and heretics who were proclaiming a distorted version of the Gospel. The sign of Christian faith was baptism. Baptism was the passing from the old order to the new. It was also the sign of the death and resurrection of Jesus, and marked the believer's union with him in a death to sin and a resurrection to new life. Through the period before Easter candidates for baptism were taught the faith and were exorcized from evil and the power of sin. They fasted and prayed. At certain stages of the church's life there may have been an insistence that the content of this preparation was kept secret. The rites were holy and of absolute significance and must not be revealed to the unbelieving world. In a sermon addressed to baptismal candidates the fourth-century catechist Cyril of Jerusalem stressed perseverance: 'Abide thou in the catechizings; though our discourse be long, let not the mind be wearied out. For thou art receiving thine armour against the antagonist's power; against heresies, against Jews and Samaritans and Gentiles.'[12]

Although the Christians looked for signs of Christ in the non-Christian world they were in no doubt that the Christian life involved warfare against evil. Baptism did not provide an automatic protection. It required a thorough resolve, a turning of heart and mind and will. Cyril could remember periods of persecution and he presents the Christian life as a life of struggle and danger in which the victory is given to those who endure.

During the reign of Constantine Christianity became one of the official religions of the empire. This was the real beginning of Christendom, when Christianity was transformed from a minority cult, tolerated but suspected, into the religion of Byzantium. Some Christians thought that the kingdom had come on earth, and that the Christian emperor was an icon of Christ the Logos.

The image of the church had changed radically. At first it was the ark of salvation, rescuing men and women out of the stormy seas of this world. Through baptism the believer passed from membership of a community heading for destruction into membership of the redeemed community: 'Thou dost bring out a vast host from the dungeon of death and, set free, they follow where their Maker goes.' That was how one ancient hymn writer[13] saw it, and the sense is echoed by the Tractarian theologian Pusey:

'See round thine ark the hungry billows curling;
See how thy foes their banners are unfurling;
Lord while their darts envenomed they are hurling,
Thou canst preserve us.'[14]

The church of the Byzantine empire was not a storm-tossed ark but a city of abundance: 'From that time on a cloudless day – a day full of light and brilliance – beams of heaven shone down on Christ's churches in every land – and no one was hesitant to invite even those outside our number to share in, if not equal benefits, at least an outpouring of and a part in the gifts God had granted us.'[15] The church at this point has become powerful. It is the munificent benefactor, the channel of God's blessing to the world. Yet in this new role the Biblical calling of the people of God has become compromised. The Church is no longer the ark of salvation, the shelter for the little flock. Its members are no longer the unclever, the uncultivated, the dispossessed. The church is no longer the witness to God's judgement in history, it has become the object of it. No one saw this with greater clarity than Augustine. His *City of God* is a devastating attack on the imperial theology. He claims that there is a distinction between the visible church with its institutional life and patterns of doctrine and worship, and the invisible Church which is rooted in eternity and is destined to be the city of God. No one can judge from an earthly perspective who are the true members of the city of God. Some members of the earthly church really belong to the city of this world. Some of those who are outside the church are true citizens. This was an extremely important development. It allowed for the possibility that the church could make mistakes. This would not contradict the promise of the guidance of the Spirit because the mistakes would manifest themselves in the fullness of time. It also meant that the church could enter a realistic dialogue with the world. The world and the church were not the same thing. There was continuity and discontinuity between them. Just as the visible church was not identical with the true Church, so the world was not identical with the city of this world, which was heading for destruction. The final judgement would only appear at the end of time. Meanwhile, it is possible, in Augustine's view, for Christians to be critical of the church while fully committed to it. It is also possible for them to take secular politics seriously, since God is fulfilling his purpose outside the church as well as inside it.

Augustine's theory offers a basic criticism of Christendom. It questions how far any human institution can reflect the divine order, even the order of the Incarnation. It returns to a much more critical stance, while having a more positive theology of the secular world than the first Christians possessed.

On the whole the Christian understanding of the relationship between the church and the state has swung between the Byzantine view and the Augustinian view.

The medieval church dominated culture; its Christian civilization was longer lived and more successful than the first attempt of Byzantium. The Reformation was in part a protest against the medieval synthesis between Christianity and culture, even though medieval culture was entirely and intentionally Christian.

In England the Reformation took a unique course. In proclaiming himself head of the English church, Henry the Eighth made himself a kind of sacred monarch. This accounts for the peculiar relationship between church and state, Christianity and culture, that we have inherited. At times the English solution has seemed closer to the optimistic Byzantine theology than to the cautious theology of Augustine. Henry the Eighth's innovation did not go unquestioned. It was, of course, a profound blasphemy to faithful Catholics; the beginning of the new era was marked by the martyrdom of Sir Thomas More. The religious claims of the monarch have been a factor in Roman Catholic apologetic against the Church of England down the centuries. It is also a factor in the movements of religious dissent in English history. The theology of monarchy can be seen quite clearly from the English Book of Common Prayer. In the accession services the divine right of the monarch over Church and state is taken for granted: 'Receive our humble prayers for our sovereign . . . as in this day set over us by thy grace and providence . . . that under him/her this nation may be wisely governed, and thy church may serve thee in all godly quietness.' The ceremonies of the coronation service are full of references to the Old Testament which lay stress on the divine election of the monarch and his special priestly role in representing the people before God:

'The King, O God, his heart to thee upraiseth;
With him the nation bows before thy face;
With high thanksgiving thee thy glad church praiseth,
Our strength thy Spirit, our trust and hope thy grace.'[16]

Our theology of monarchy has combined conveniently with our national aspirations over the centuries. Our long period of political stability and our successes in colonial adventures abroad gave credence to the half-believed idea that God had a special relationship with England, analagous to the original covenant with Israel. The popularity of the hymn 'Jerusalem' with Blake's haunting words and Parry's triumphant tune bears witness to this strand in English religious life. But our theology of the sacred state has always been questioned by Roman Catholics and non-conformists. There were revivals of dissenting protest at the time of the present Queen's Silver Jubilee celebrations when a form of service was sent to churches of all denominations with a mandate that it should be used by them. Even Anglicans registered a sense of unease at this trespassing by the monarch on religious freedom. Because, of course, in practice the monarch does not play a significant part in church affairs. In the same way that we have developed what is in practice a secular constitution and a democratic means of government, the theology of divine election only hovers on as a hangover from the past to be invoked occasionally by those who are nostalgic for Christendom. Still, the memory of Christendom is tenacious because it *has* been such a real part of our national life. As often happens it is outside the church of committed believers that the memory is strongest, among those who, as Lord Blake put it: 'Think in the tradition even if they are not active exponents.'

But what of the committed believers and their stance in the world today? We have already seen a variety of different responses. There is the false response which looks for the return of Christendom. There is also the weak response, when the church plods along quietly in the wake of secularism, accepting the insights of the secular world without question. So we may judge the flabbiness of the Church on the issue of religious education; having been pushed out of its dominating role the church has simply acquiesced in a form of religious teaching which appears 'objective' and 'value-free' but is, in fact, loaded with assumptions which may be, at times, anti-Christian.

The Biblical images which describe the people of God never suggest that it is important how many they are or how successful they are being. The only thing that seems to matter is that the community is faithful to its calling. So the New Testament uses the image of salt – the salt that is scattered and seasons society, bringing out its true flavour. If the salt loses its saltiness then society loses the benefit. The church has a responsibility not to be conformed to the world. At the same time the church is not to seek power. This is brought out most strikingly in the Old Testament image of the Servant of the Lord. The servant is humiliated and unattractive in the world's eyes. The imagery is harsh and it portrays one who bears the sickness and unwholeness of the rest of the community. His origins are unpromising, his career is anything but successful. But he is unswervingly faithful to his task, which is to suffer without any of the normal human securities. He also, at least in one of the Servant songs, suffers in silence. He has no message for those who attack him, no glib answer for those who look for one. In the New Testament the image of the servant is applied to Christ. The self-emptying of God in Christ, and his willingness to be humiliated, to suffer and die, sets an example for Christians to follow,[17] as the Epistle to the Philippians makes clear.

It is sometimes assumed that language of divine Incarnation leads to a kind of social triumphalism. Because of the Incarnation all that is human is holy, and the institutions of Christianity take on immense significance. Some writers have asserted that the whole paraphernalia of 'Christendom' can be traced to the Incarnation doctrine.[18]

Yet the Biblical images do not allow for a triumphalistic understanding of the Incarnation. God is the one who 'pitches his tent among us', not the one who leads us to build immense cathedrals. Incarnation language in the Bible stresses the grace and vulgarity of God, not the triumphs of man. If these images are applied to the church which is now the Body of Christ in the world it should be clear that they lead to a humble and realistic assessment of the role of the people of God. The people of God are a minority in society. They are not themselves 'the saved' or the only 'saved'; God saves whom he will. But they carry the news of salvation. The news of salvation is not only religious news. It is also news about the nature of man and society. But the church cannot share this news, or even have access to it, until it has learnt the gift of discernment. The discernment of spirits is vital for any realistic understanding of culture. It is especially necessary for those who work in education. The spirits are the powers for good or evil which are present to the church through culture and society. Christians have an absolute responsibility to bear witness to inhumanity, to whatever threatens to disfigure the image of God in man. They should be aware of the subtlety with which these forces can creep into our human systems and structures unnoticed. They will be aware, with shame of the times when the church has not noticed them.

The church also has a responsibility to develop 'the Christian mind'. If the time comes when the educational process is leading in a direction that contradicts the image of God in man, then Christians should be considering alternative means of education. At any rate they must assess the value of church schools and Sunday schools and consider how adequate they are in their attempts to offer a Christian education. They should also look seriously at the provision for the teaching of adult Christians, which in most churches is minimal.

It is not the job of the state schools to make Christians, and to think this is a hangover of nostalgia for Christian civilization, which is a form of idolatry.

Christians can hope of a secular state that it will be a secular state, not drawing to itself the trappings of a sacred state, but working for the free development of the individual and for understanding between different cultural and social groups. If these are the aims of the secular state and the education system which it implements, Christians need have no quarrel with it. The discernment of spirits can lead Christians to choose liberal values, as long as they realize that they are just that, liberal values, and as much under the judgement of God as any other set of values. The teaching of religion has an important function in education, and it is possible that it may become a safeguard against the false objectivity and nihilism which has penetrated our culture. But it will only have this function if those who teach it avoid the false dichotomy between science and experience which some of the syllabuses promote. This is an area for Christian witness, but it has nothing directly to do with making Christians. It is a witness to the image of God in man.

It is though, the job of the churches to make and sustain Christians, to help them to realize the elements of continuity and discontinuity between faith and culture, and to sharpen their understanding for the critical task of bearing their witness in society.

In doing this the churches must rediscover their resources in Biblical theology and prayer, and must be conscious of the dangers of introverted emotionalism and vapid liberalism, the snare of political power and the seduction of humanistic secularism. Only if these resources are rediscovered will Christians be able to distinguish the guidance of the Spirit, calling the church to involvement or disengagement, to acceptance and celebration, or to repentance and questioning.

NOTES

1. *Young People's Beliefs*: p. 24
2. Ibid.
3. Richard G. Jones in *100 Hymns for Today*, William Clowes & Sons Ltd, 1969
4. *Education, Nihilism and Survival*: David Holbrook, Darton Longman & Todd 1977, p. 3
5. Ibid. p. 7
6. Ibid. p. 22
7. 'Christianity and British Civilization': Lord Blake in *Curriculum Christianity*, Unity Press, March 1977, p. 9
8. See *The New Demons*: Jacques Ellul, Mowbrays 1977
9. I Corinthians I:26-27, Revised Standard Version
10. *The Epistle to the Romans*: Karl Barth, trans. Edwyn C. Hoskyns, Oxford, 1968 (paperback ed.), p. 35
11. *The Buddha*: Trevor Ling, Pelican 1973, p. 29
12. *Lectures on the Christian Sacraments*: St Cyril of Jerusalem, trans. R. W. Church for the library of the Fathers, SPCK, 1951, p. 46
13. Easter hymns by Venantius Fortunatus
14. P. Pusey: 'Lord of our Life and God of our Salvation'
15. From *Ecclesiastic History* of Eusebius
16. Yattendon Hymnal
17. Philippians 2:5-11
18. Especially and most convincingly in 'The Christ of Christendom': Don Cupitt in *The Myth of God Incarnate*, SCMP 1977, pp. 133 ff

CHAPTER SEVEN

Education and the Christian Mind

This chapter is really a postscript. It is not about teaching religion in the classroom but continues as the last chapter ended, with a discussion of the task of the Church. If the church is modelled on the image of the Servant in a society that styles itself 'secular', 'pluralist', or 'Christian', then the church has a formidable educational task among its own members. Yet how successful is the church in making Christians? How far are Christians equipped to offer a critique of culture? Is the church itself able to discern the spirits? 'There is no longer a Christian mind. It is a commonplace that the mind of modern man has been secularized. For instance, it has been deprived of any orientation towards the supernatural. Tragic as this fact is, it would not be so desperately tragic had the Christian mind held out against the secular drift. But unfortunately the Christian mind has succumbed to the secular drift with a degree of weakness and nervelessness unmatched in Christian history.'[1]

The Christian mind is a mind that has responded in faith to the Christian message and seeks a unity of feeling and critical intelligence. The Christian mind accepts the tension of living in two worlds, of trying to make sense of the secular in the light of the age to come. The Christian mind needs to develop. It forms gradually as the individual matures as a human being and his prayer life grows deep and stable. The foundations of the Christian mind can be laid in childhood. Yet there is not much evidence that the church is concerned with this in its ministry to children. There are historical reasons for this. The Sunday School Movement developed during the industrial revolution. The aim was to teach children, whose families often belonged to no particular church, the rudiments of reading, writing and religion. Often in their history, Sunday schools have functioned quite separately from the worshipping congregations of particular churches. Parents have sent children to Sunday schools partly to get them out of the way for a few hours, partly in the hope that a dose of religion might do them some good. In some churches this pattern of separation between worship and Sunday school continues. In others there have been attempts at integration. Many non-conformist churches let the children attend the beginning of the service and then send them off to their classes after a children's hymn and an address. In the Anglican churches the popularity of the parish communion has raised complex questions of whether children should receive a blessing at the altar rail while the adults are receiving communion. Arising out of these practical questions are deeper ones about the Christian understanding of the family and of childhood. It is obvious that Christian parents have a responsibility for teaching their children about Christianity. It is in the family that the child first learns to relate to other people, and to develop a sense of his individual worth. As he grows older he will respond to his parents' attitude. If their profession of faith clearly means something to them in *their* everyday life he will be aware that it is real to them. If their attitude at home contradicts their behaviour in church he will be suspicious.

It is certainly true that the church supports the institution of the family and regards it as the most important unit for passing on the Christian life. Yet the church's motive for supporting the family seems to be political rather than religious and to be lacking in critical awareness. Frequently Christian leaders support family life on the grounds that it makes for a stable society. The church has regarded motherhood as woman's chief vocation, and has exalted it into a quasi-sacred function. The modern

church particularly accepts the idolization of children
without question. The world is child-centred, so is the
church. So the 'family-service' becomes the most important
service of the week. Mothering Sunday and Christmas
are sacred days of the family, when, predictably, the
churches are full of families who otherwise rarely attend.

Yet there is no evidence in the New Testament that the
family is a particularly important unit for the transmission
of the Christian faith. The gospels seem to show, in contrast, that Christian life often involves a rejection of the
family and the family's values. The church traditionally
has valued the single life as a genuine alternative. The
single person in the church should be regarded as a free
person, not as a failure. Yet the church today colludes
with society in rejecting the single person, the widow or
widower and the homosexual:

'We hurry to church in all kinds of weather
Sunday's the day we can all be together
Mummies and Daddies and children and grans
Even the babies we bring in their prams.'[2]

The family service effectively sabotages any attempt
to give serious Christian teaching to either adults or
children in the context of worship. Sermons have to be
understood by the youngest child present. They must,
therefore, be short and jolly. The clergyman taking the
service becomes a family entertainer running a weekly
show which confirms the heresy that the Western nuclear
family is God's pattern for human society: 'All too rarely
has it (the family service) been subject to searching and
discriminating theological enquiry. It chimed in with the
contemporary mood too easily and too well . . .'[3]

Such an enquiry might put the family back in perspective. It would at any rate be a beginning for the Christian
critique of contemporary culture which is so lacking. It
would also mean that the teaching of adults and children

could be looked at afresh, as the different exercises that they are.

There are, of course, outlines for Sunday school work available for the churches, and to these we now turn. What is the purpose of Sunday school? Many churches adhere to the evangelical pattern, and believe that the aim is to bring children to personal faith in Christ. The Scripture Union offer a number of outlines, most of which are heavily Bible-based. Each lesson includes a Bible passage to be studied. There is also often a short passage to be learnt by heart. Songs and choruses are provided. One booklet, *Teaching 7-10's*, suggests a rather unintelligent collection of Bible stories, including the story of Potiphar's wife and her attempt to seduce Joseph, which seems curious material for seven year olds. Each lesson has an aim, which is made clear for the teacher's benefit. For example: 'To show the children the importance of standing up for Jesus, and of being unashamed of having faith in him', and: 'To teach the children that God is patient; he wants us to be sorry and willing to change our ways and does not "give us up" '.[4]

The trained teacher looking through the material offered by the Scripture Union may have the impression that the authors are not very aware of the insights of educational psychology in showing how children learn. This does not in itself condemn the authors, since the conclusions of the psychologists should always be open to question and revision. Yet there is something disturbing about the way one author, Margaret V. Old, replaces all educational insight with a simplistic appeal to the power of revelation: 'There are people who argue that since the religious ideas a child is able to express verbally often sound crude he is not "ready for religion" until he moves beyond thinking in concrete terms and is able to discuss abstract ideas ... Religion, however, is not at all the same as Christianity, and religious thinking is not at all the same as an encounter with the living Christ ... We need to remem-

ber that the Holy Spirit who inspired it (the Bible) is still
active in giving spiritual perception and understanding
that are not the same thing as the developing mind's
ability to reason and comprehend.'[5]

This argument falls down theologically because it is so
notoriously unconcerned for the child's wholeness. It is
true that children can make a response of faith. But that
response has to deepen and grow. It will never grow if
it is located in the past, in some childhood conversion
which has been regarded as separate from the rest of the
child's development. With the onset of intellectual and
emotional maturity the child may reject Christianity
because it has been fixed in him as part of his immaturity.
The evangelical approach as represented here can do little
to lay the foundations of a Christian mind.

The British Council of Churches takes a very different
line in its booklet *The Child in the Church*.[6] Here the
argument is that the aim of Christian nurture is to help
the child to develop to the point where he can make a
decision for or against faith. The authors seem to see the
Sunday school as continuing and extending the policy
of the secular school with regard to RE. They make the
familiar distinction between education and instruction,
not being favourably disposed toward the latter, and con-
demning outright what they term indoctrination. There
is no attempt to make a Christian assessment of the
liberal assumptions of county school religion; indeed it
is assumed that such liberalism is the natural fruit of
Christianity. The booklet accepts the child-centredness of
today's society, and finds theological justification for
continuing this pattern in the church by quoting the
story in the gospels of Jesus taking children in his arms
and blessing them. Such an approach seems to me to be,
frankly, a sell-out to the spirit of the age: 'A close look
at some of the current pressures on the Church in the
name of family worship might well quickly lay bare
splurges of sentimental emotionalism clustered round the

enthroned child.'[7] The authors are clearly sincere and thoughtful Christians though it is no surprise to learn that some of them are, in fact, thorough going proponents of the new RE in schools. *The Child in the Church* does not include any teaching material, but its assumptions are beginning to have an effect on the kind of material being produced.

Partners in Learning is a church community education programme produced by the Methodist church:[8] 'The process of living is a constant interplay between our contemporary experience and our faith.' The programme consists of teaching outlines for all ages, from three to adulthood. It seeks a mid-point between Bible-based and experience-based teaching. Yet this worthy aim leads to some strange misuses of Biblical material. Perhaps it is unfair to quote from a lesson intended for three to four year olds, but it is so extraordinary that it should be examined. The aim of the lesson is: 'To help the children see that where there is trust there is no need for conflict.' After some games with play dough and dominoes and a session of 'follow my leader' the teacher invites all the children to sit down. There will be a commotion as the children jostle one another in their eagerness to sit next to the teacher. The teacher explains that the children are behaving just like the friends of Jesus. He then tells a version of what I can only assume is the story in chapter twenty of St Matthew's gospel, where the mother of James and John requests that her sons should sit next to Jesus in the glory of the kingdom. In the New Testament version the story is about priority in the kingdom. James and John feel they have a claim to special honour. They say that they are willing to share the cup of suffering that lies ahead for Jesus. Jesus prophesies that they will share in his sufferings, but there is no guarantee that they will ensure for themselves places of honour in the kingdom. The other disciples are angry at the presumption of James and John and there follows a section of teaching in which Jesus explains that the scrambling for position and honour which is taken for granted among the gentiles should be rejected by the disciples. In the kingdom the order of honour is reversed. Those who are honoured are those who have not pushed themselves forward, but have been humble and patient towards others.

Here is the children's version as proposed by *Partners in Learning*: 'James and John thought they would make sure that they sat next to Jesus, so they asked their mother to go and ask Jesus if they could. She came to where Jesus was and said, "Please can my sons sit next to you at the party?"

'Jesus knew about all the quarrelling that was going on, so he said to them all, "I know you would all like to sit next to me, but it is not necessary to quarrel about it. You are all my friends, and I love you all, so you will all have a turn to sit by me."

'Then the friends were happy because they knew that Jesus loved them all.'

It is possible, of course, that the author of this outline did not know the story in Matthew's gospel, and so made this up as fiction. It is anyway about as complete a distortion of the original as can be conceived. Matthew's version is about insecurity. The kingdom implies a radical transformation of human values. The children's version is a pious little fable about the love of Jesus. It could be argued that the original story is hardly suitable for three year olds. But that does not excuse the re-working of the story to prove the exact opposite of what it originally meant. To misuse the Bible in this way is hardly to encourage a mature grappling with the Biblical message in adulthood.

Both the Scripture Union outlines and the *Partners in Learning* programme raise serious questions about using the Bible with young children. Yet one of the most successful courses for children does not use the Bible at all. This is a course of experimental lessons worked out by

Roman Catholic catechists.[9] This course does not demand a mature commitment of faith, nor does it patronize. It is experientially based, but it follows up experience with clear and informative teaching. The approach seems to spring from the belief that, for the children going to the classes, Christian faith is a fulfilment of personality, and that it will be part of their development as whole human beings. The teaching is neither indoctrinatory, nor vacuous. It is only in this course, which is not yet generally available, that there is anything approaching a concern for the development of the Christian mind.

One place where it might be thought the Christian mind could be discovered is in university departments of theology. Theology is a problematic word. Once the word denoted 'the queen of sciences', now it is a word that can be used by politicians to denote specious reasoning. The word theology in fact means the science of God, and traditionally its subject matter was God, as he has revealed himself in history, scripture and tradition. Yet modern theologians are uneasy with this approach. When Maurice Wiles, the Regius Professor of Divinity at Oxford considers the question 'What is theology?' he admits that: 'Much of the theologian's time will be taken up with historical and sociological studies of what has been believed in the past, and what is believed now . . .'[10] Theology today has to compete with other subjects such as history, science and sociology. How can it make sense of the claim that its subject matter is God?

Professor Wiles is not sure about this. As he sees it, the bulk of the theologian's time will be taken up with historical, literary and sociological studies. He has to come to an understanding of the Biblical texts as literature of their time. He may have to learn the Biblical languages. He will need something of a historian's skills to make sense of the historical context of his study, and to assess the evidence about the growth and development of the Christian church. If he is considering religion today he may find himself using the tools of anthropology or sociology. Is there anything which pulls all these different skills together? Professor Wiles finds no single strand running through them all, no all-embracing, coherent principle. He does feel, however, that the issue can, and should, be discussed, and that is also part of the theologian's task. So theologians become rather like the characters in Beckett's play *Waiting for Godot*, carrying out a number of incomplete, unrelated dialogues in the vague hope that a unifying principle might emerge. Yet for Professor Wiles this is the only way theology can avoid a ghetto existence. He believes that theology is relevant to everyone and must be in free and open dialogue with other academic disciplines. It might seem that Professor Wiles is really advocating a change from theology to religious studies, that is, to the discipline which regards religion as a human phenomenon to be studied without presuppositions as to its value or truth. Many university departments have already made this shift. It is part of the secularization of religious teaching which we have been concerned with in the schools. Yet Professor Wiles is not entirely happy with this position. While finding religious studies a useful tool for the theologian he is still convinced that the disciplines are different. By its very nature theology will appeal to those who have considerable sympathy with the Christian faith. This is not necessarily true of religious studies. Theology also differs because it has an impact on the church. The theologian in the university has a responsibility to the church. He is concerned with testing the truth claims made by the church and helping the church to interpret and elucidate the Christian faith for today.

The problem is whether these two roles can be held together any more. Who is the theologian responsible to, the university or the church? When the Christian faith was the faith of the university there was no real conflict. But now it seems probable that there is no place for 'theology' as such in the university today. So the theologian has to become an expert in religious studies, primarily Christian ones, or lose his academic credibility. Yet this new approach to theology has little to do with building the Christian mind. Its orientation is self-consciously secular. When the theologians *do* speak to the church they merely reinforce the message of rationalist reductionism which is present throughout society. The church, on the whole, remains suspicious of and hostile towards the theologian who seems so set on dissecting and explaining away the faith of the ordinary Christian. Yet the academic establishment does not seem unduly impressed by the attempts of theologians to make themselves academically respectable.

Dr Eric Mascall is sharply critical of what he sees as a sell-out on the part of the university theologians: 'For some (theologians) it seems to be the only way in which, under increased economic stringency and increased dependence upon state assistance in a secularized society, theology can achieve some manner and degree of survival. For some it seems to offer a wider scope for the claim of theology to be an academically respectable discipline. For some, in whom theological delinquence has reached an advanced condition, it reflects their own loss of conviction that Christianity is in any important sense unique.'[11]

The decline in theology in the universities would not be so tragic if there was evidence that the church was maintaining a tradition of theological teaching elsewhere. But this does not seem to be happening. The churches' theological colleges, apart from the fundamentalist ones, tend to build close links with university departments of theology. Their theological training does not differ very much from what is taught in the universities. Theology suffers from a lack of morale even among candidates for the ministry, who too often conclude that it is irrelevant to the real issues they will confront in the future. They

may be encouraged to share the assumption that theology
is really a set of unrelated disciplines looking for some
kind of unifying principle. Some students find that there
is little attempt at theological college to integrate study
with prayer and worship. Now, there must be a real and
healthy tension between study and prayer. Study sharpens
and deepens prayer, prayer humanizes study. Study must
raise criticisms, doubts and arguments; prayer must wrestle
with these and find meaning in them. But all too often
prayer and study are regarded as totally separate. Many
colleges make little effort to teach prayer at all. It is
regarded as private to the individual. Spiritual direction
is replaced by some form of 'counselling'. Valuable and
necessary though this may be it is not the same thing.
The student may well emerge from theological college
without having integrated prayer with study and commitment. The attempt to build the Christian mind has
failed. Once again the church reflects and does not
challenge the schizoid splits between thought and feeling,
private and public, which dominate society.

And yet we come back to the question 'what is
theology?' Karl Barth accepted the value of Biblical
criticism and language study. But for him these were
ancillary disciplines. They were useful and important,
but only insofar as they shed light on the real issue of
theology: 'Theology stands and falls with the Word of
God, for the Word of God precedes all theological words
by creating, arousing, and challenging them.'[12]

Barth starts by assuming that theology is concerned
with the speech of God. He accepts, therefore, that the
Christian God is a God who speaks and whose speech can
be apprehended, however, dimly, by man. Not all
theologians would share these assumptions, but it seems
to me that a theology which does not recognize them as
a starting point has really ceased to be Christian. For
Barth, theological existence is characterized by wonder,
concern, commitment and faith. In other words it is a

response. Theological work includes prayer, service and love as well as study. So the theologian is first and foremost an interpreter of the Word. His first responsibility is to the community called into existence by the Word, the Christian Church. His activity cannot be separated from the work and worship of the church. The theologian must be a man of prayer. He searches himself for a unity between thinking and feeling, criticism and sympathy.

Dr Mascall claims that real theology: 'Is fundamentally concerned with the same theme as the church's pastoral ministry, namely, the redemption and glorification of man by God his creator through the passion, death and resurrection of Jesus Christ, the incarnate son.'[13]

There are two disturbing results for the churches from the decline of theology. The first is the revival of Biblical fundamentalism. It is easy to see how this has arisen, especially in the student world. The would-be theological student finds himself engaged in a bit of textual criticism, a dash of sociology and so on. This is presented with no unifying principle behind it. It seems to have little relation to his Christian commitment. He feels instinctively that Christianity involves a degree of discontinuity with culture. He assumes, not without justification, that his teachers are steeped in the assumptions of the world. He comes to distrust the compromise with secularism. In fundamentalism he finds authority. He finds the unifying principle that was missing from his studies. He accepts that the Bible is infallible and inerrant. He experiences a new unity of mind and heart. Unfortunately, it is a false unity, based on sub-Christian presuppositions. But by this stage fundamentalism has taken over. For it does not only offer a theology. It is a religious culture in its own right offering a complete vocabulary and world perspective. Many find in it a kind of wholeness which the rest of the church does not seem able to offer.

But in the end Christianity is not a religion of a book. Islam is, and there is religious logic in the Muslim belief

in the infallibility of the Koran. Christianity, however, is
a religion of the Word, and the Word is not circumscribed
by words, even the words of the Bible. The Word is God's
Word, active in creation and human history, and,
supremely, in the life, death and resurrection of Jesus
Christ. To treat the Bible as the Word is to make an idol
of it. The words of the Bible are theology, they are words
of witness and response to the activity of the Word. Yet
the fundamentalist movement is significant for Christianity
and for the churches' witness today. No one was more
aware of this than Karl Barth. Barth belonged to the
Calvinist tradition and, at times, he wrote warmly of
the doctrine of verbal inspiration. For the doctrine kept
alive the insight that God is a God who speaks. Fundamentalism does that today, and its success is a measure
of the rest of the church's failure to respond to the Word
of God.

The second consequence of the decline of theology is
the ever-yawning gap between theologians and ordinary
clergy, and between academically-minded clergy and
ordinary Christians. There is a double loss here. It means
that the ordinary Christian has no awareness of the
borderlands of theology, like Biblical criticism. This is a
pity, because it makes him vulnerable to the temptation
to take scripture literally, even without the fundamentalist
philosophy behind it. It has recently been pointed out
that even after several hundred years of general scholarly
consensus, many ordinary Christians would not regard
St John's gospel as being any different from the other
three.[14] At the same time ordinary Christians without
any knowledge of Biblical criticism frequently reject
scripture just because it is incredible. The beginning of
Genesis, or the miracle stories in the New Testament seem
unbelievable so the layman rejects them. He is not helped
to see that they still carry immense theological significance, a significance which becomes clearer once it is
realized that they should *not* necessarily be regarded as

historical. Or the lay person might come across the idea that the gospels, far from being biographies of Jesus, are written out of the faith of the early church. But he does not see this as significant for the church, rather, it just confirms his suspicion that the gospels are inaccurate and cannot be trusted. This does not turn him away from the church, but it means that his Christian faith affects him less and less as a whole person. He remains sentimentally attached to Jesus, and habitually used to church-going, but there is no intellectual core to his faith.

The churches do contain a very large number of intelligent laymen and women, who exercise considerable intellectual skill in their daily work, and yet who are never challenged to apply their minds to their faith. Their grasp of Christianity remains childish and stunted. There is a kind of schizophrenia. The intelligent layman puts his intelligence aside as soon as he enters a church, and, unfortunately is often encouraged to do so.

Coming at the problem from a different direction, Fr Kenneth Leech has written recently about the lack of spiritual direction in the churches.[15] By this he means that there are few who are competent to guide and advise others in the life of prayer. This is hardly surprising, as it is only recently that prayer has become respectable again. At the time of *Honest to God* Christian prayer was widely regarded as impossible. Rather than attempt a disciplined prayer life Christians were encouraged to cultivate 'depth' in their attitudes to work and relationships. Contemplation, intercession and adoration had no functional value, and so were seen as an escape from reality. Now the tide has turned, and many Christians are searching for spiritual guidance. In their search for wholeness, for integration between thought and feeling, not a few have sought guidance outside the Christian tradition. Yet, as Fr Leech points out, prayer and spiritual direction have never been regarded as an optional extra of the Christian life. Prayer is the heart of the Christian life. It is anything but a pious withdrawal from the world. It is rather an attempt to grapple with the world, and its sufferings, in the light of the age to come. Prayer is the bridge between the two worlds that the Christian has to live in. Without it there is no wholeness. He remains a divided being.

This chapter has, on the whole, painted a rather gloomy picture. The church does not seem to be making a very effective job of educating its members for witness in today's society. It is not that churchmen are not concerned. They are, and particularly with the education of children. It was out of this concern that the Education Board of the General Synod of the Church of England invited two sociologically-trained researchers to conduct a survey into the beliefs held by young people.[16] I have already quoted from this survey, which is remarkable for the candour of response from the interviewees and its uniformity. For what emerged with overwhelming clarity is that young people imagine religion to be a wholly private matter. None of those asked considered that religion had any relevance for their social lives or that it might affect the choices they made in life. Only for a few did religion have any bearing on moral issues. The church was despised by everyone, except by a small group who had been influenced by the Jesus movement. Those who went to church were hypocrites and swots. Yet all claimed that tolerance was important, and declared their own tolerance for all points of view. They found little value in the teaching of religion or in religious institutions: 'Those who described themselves as believers in something recognizably related to conventional Christian terms went on to display varieties of inconsistency, doubt, unbelief, superstition; and those who declared themselves unbelievers almost always went on to indicate some uncertainty, some attraction to this or that belief or superstition or so on.'

These teenagers and young adults with their honesty

and muddle are the products of our culture. They are reflecting back exactly what has been fed to them through their parents, through school, through the media, through their peer-group. The fact that some of them go to church or regard themselves as believers makes little difference to their basic paganism. This is because the church, as we have seen, shares and reflects the assumptions of the world.

But there are signs of hope. Not in the teaching of children yet. But there are increasing numbers of adult Christians who are concerned for wholeness, for whom the Christian religion has again become a way of salvation. There are groups that meet to pray together and explore silence. There are evening classes in Bible topics and worship. There is always a danger that these activities will be split off from the rest of life, that they will be yet another symptom of the disease rather than the beginning of a cure. But there has to be some point at which theology and experience are brought together. In Christian tradition this centre-ing is prayer. To some, the idea of an inner life, a prayer life, sounds reactionary. It sounds like an opting-out, a return to a ghetto mentality. But that is because the jargon of the time condemns ghettoes. But it does exalt community. And, whereas communities should be open-ended, they need a core and a centre of shared belief and experience in order to be a community at all. It is a long time since a majority of Christians have given serious attention to the challenge: ' "Come out from them and be separate from them," says the Lord.' And yet the point of turning from the world to God is to encounter the world *in* God. The separation comes from discernment, and it is the way to a real dialogue and a real commitment.

Time and again we have seen how in one area, that of education, the church has either clung on to some faded vision of power and influence or shuffled along in a spineless procession in the direction carved out by those motivated by philosophies hostile to Christianity.

It is unthinkable that Christians should opt out of the world and the struggles for meaning in the world. They are called always to involvement as parents, teachers, educationists, as writers and television producers. But their involvement will be worthless unless they are prepared to rediscover the depths of their own tradition. They cannot speak as Christians until they have discovered the mind of Christ.

The absence of the Christian mind is reflected in the sad fact that the best known lay Christian today is Mrs Mary Whitehouse. With her simplistic fundamentalism and Moral Re-armament background she crusades for a form of Christendom which is the antithesis of the searching and suffering of the kingdom.

What is needed is a deeper assessment which neither totally accepts nor totally rejects the world, but struggles to see it through the mind of Christ, and bring to it authentic judgement and authentic hope. This assessment can only be made by a church that has renounced power, that is repentant for the sins of the past, and has its roots in theology and prayer, the two responses to the Word of God. Only to the extent to which the church deepens its roots in God will it have anything to share with the world at all.

NOTES

1. *The Christian Mind*: Harry Blamires, SPCK 1963, p. 3
2. *New Child Songs*: National Christian Education Council, Denholm House Press 1973
3. 'Problems and Perspectives': Neville Clark in *Worship and the Child*, the Joint Liturgical Group, SPCK 1975, p. 12
4. *Teaching 7-10s*, January-March 1977: Scripture Union 1977, pp. 16, 37
5. *Today's Children, Tomorrow's Church*: Margaret V. Old, Scripture Union 1974, pp. 31-2

6. *The Child in the Church* : British Council of Churches, 1976
7. 'Problems and Perspectives' : *Worship and the Child*, p. 12
8. *Partners in Learning* : Part 2, February-June 1978, Methodist Church Division of Education and Youth, and National Christian Education Council, April 1977
9. *Experimental Lessons in Catechetics* : The Grail, Pinner, p. 19
10. *What is Theology?* Maurice Wiles, Oxford 1976, pp. 6, 7
11. *Theology and The Gospel of Christ* : E. L. Mascall, SPCK 1977, p. 19
12. *Evangelical Theology: An Introduction* : Karl Barth, trans. Grover Foley, Collins/Fontana 1965, pp. 20, 21
13. *Theology and the Gospel of Christ* : p. 23
14. *The Unexamined Assumption of Most Christian Believers* : R. Hanson in *The Times*, 10 June 1978
15. *Soulfriend* : Kenneth Leech, Sheldon Press 1977
16. *Young People's Beliefs*

For Further Reading

The Classroom

Teenage Religion, by Harold Loukes, SCMP 1961
Teaching Religion in Schools, by Jean Holm, OUP 1975
What Can I do in RE? by Michael Grimmitt, Mayhew
   McCrimmon 1973

Worship

School Worship – An Obituary, by John Hull, SCMP 1975
Worship and the Child, the Joint Liturgical Group,
   SPCK 1975

Theology

The Christian in Education, by Colin Alves, SCMP 1970
The Fourth 'R', the Durham Report on Religious Education, SPCK 1970

Religious Politics

The Idea of a Christian Society, by T. S. Eliot, Faber and Faber 1939

The New Demons, by Jacques Ellul, Mowbrays 1977

Education, Nihilism and Survival, by David Holbrook, Darton Longman and Todd 1977

Tracts Against the Times, by David Martin, Lutterworth Press 1977

Also available in Fount Paperbacks

The Religious Experience of Mankind
NINIAN SMART

'. . . quite masterly. In the space of two pages he covers most of the relevant details of totemism and taboo in a way that conveys information to the general reader clearly and succinctly . . . should whet the reader's appetite to study further, and it contains an admirable bibliography.'   *Glasgow Herald*

Evil and the God of Love
JOHN HICK

'. . . the tone of this book is magnificent. It is the most exciting work of its kind that I have read for several years.'
                                        John Raymond, Sunday Times

Wrestling with Christ
LUIGI SANTUCCI

'This is a most unusual book, a prolonged meditation of the life of Christ using many changing literary forms, dialogue, description, addresses to Christ, passages of self-communing. It is written by a Christian passionately concerned that everyone should know Jesus Christ.'   *Catholic Herald*

Journey for a Soul
GEORGE APPLETON

'Wherever you turn in this inexpensive but extraordinarily valuable paperback you will benefit from sharing this man's pilgrimage of the soul.'   *Methodist Recorder*

Also available in Fount Paperbacks

A Historical Introduction to the New Testament
ROBERT GRANT

'This splendid book is a New Testament introduction with a difference . . . All students of the New Testament will welcome this original and courageous study.'
Professor James S. Stewart

The Historical Geography of the Holy Land
G. ADAM SMITH

'A classic which has fascinated and instructed generations of students. This masterpiece among the vast literature on the Bible . . . will continue to delight readers as well as to inform.'
H. H. Rowley

The Dead Sea Scrolls 1947-1969
EDMUND WILSON

'A lucid narrative of the discovery of the scrolls which soon turns into a learned detective story; then an account of the excitement, the consternation and the intrigues.'
V. S. Pritchett, New Statesman

The Gospels and the Jesus of History
XAVIER LEON-DUFOUR

'This book is far more than an introduction to the study of the Gospels. With its detailed study of the Gospels and of the other New Testament books it is an excellent introduction to the Christology of the New Testament.'
William Barclay